More praise for *Creating the Vital Organization*

"This book presents an easy to understand paradigm for bringing balance and vitality to your organization, using a mixture of data, true to life stories, and commonsense. The practical approach it offers is tremendously insightful. It's a valuable addition to any OD practitioner's library."

—Carrie Speckart, Associate Director of Human Resources,
The Trust for Public Land

"Reading *Creating the Vital Organization* excited me as the director of a nonprofit homeless services organization. It gave me a simple framework of balancing Current Performance with Future Potential. As nonprofit leaders we are so often immersed in the day to day struggles of our organizations. Now I know I need to take time for future planning to create optimum organizational vitality."

—Terrie Light, Executive Director, Berkeley Food and Housing Project

Creating the Vital Organization

Balancing Short-Term Profits with Long-Term Success

Scott M. Brooks • *Jeffrey M. Saltzman*

Scott M. Brooks
San Fransisco, California, USA

Jeffrey M. Saltzman
New York, USA

ISBN 978-1-137-53692-1   ISBN 978-1-137-53694-5   (eBook)
DOI 10.1057/978-1-137-53694-5

Library of Congress Control Number: 2016936725

Cover illustration: © yganko / iStock / Thinkstock

Printed on acid-free paper

This Palgrave Macmillan imprint is published by Springer Nature
The registered company is Springer Nature America Inc. New York

This book is dedicated to Barbara, my wife and friend, and my daughter Audrey, whose own work ethic drove me to finish this book. Thank you for putting up with a lot of absenteeism from me so that I could write. And in memory of those close to me whom I lost during this process: Lucy Saltzman, my mom (1925–2015); and my sister-in-law, Louise Wescott (1965–2015).
—*Jeffrey Saltzman*

I am in continuous awe of my wife Emily for all she does to encourage and support my variously intense and distracting professional pursuits. This book is dedicated to her and to my boys Zander, Zach, and Mitch, whose own journeys have inspired deeper thinking into the concepts of balancing Current Performance and Future Potential.
—*Scott Brooks*

Acknowledgements

The authors would like to thank Victoria Hendrickson—insightful commenter throughout the process, researcher, and chronicler of the history of Vitality and Ambidexterity, and Amanda May Dundas—editor extraordinaire who made magic with words. Thanks to Laurie Harting, executive editor at Palgrave, who believed in our work and made this happen.

Thanks also to Julian Allen, who was able to find any article and research fact needed, Hanna Lerner who answered all of our questions about justice and constitutions, and Edwin Kuo who created compelling model designs. Thanks also to Michelle Turchin and Corrine Donovan for their thoughtful commenting on early drafts. And Walter Reichman, who knows a thing or two, and taught us about perseverance. A special thank you to the various executives who agreed to be interviewed, including Gary Stich, Cristián Samper, Jade Augustine, and John Cavelli. Also to various Friday Group members who allowed Jeff to present the book concepts at meetings and offered helpful commentary. Thanks also to Jeff's colleagues at Binghamton University, who keep him intellectually stimulated and invited to stimulating events—Kim Jaussi, Fran Yammarino, Shelly Dionne, and Upinder Dhillon, and to his MBA students who volunteered to share their experiences in implementing the concepts in this book.

Finally, we absolutely need to acknowledge the amazing staff at our company OrgVitality, who helped us to manage substantial growth during the year of writing this book, and those who inspire us by embodying the very essence of Vitality—getting things done while simultaneously building the future.

Contents

List of Figures

List of Tables

CHAPTER 1

Introduction

In your organization, do you focus on streamlining Current Performance—squeezing more output from your resources, shaving costs, or pressing for speed—or do you step back from the day-to-day and consider the future of your business, including what kinds of products and services your team or business need to provide in the future? Clearly, attention to both is necessary, but each is a distinct pursuit: They require different skills and resources, different ways to evaluate success, and even different time horizons to know if you are on the right track. It is a challenge to focus on both daily and future needs, and especially to have to constantly switch your attention between the two. Often, in the battle between daily needs and future concerns, it is the consideration of the future that suffers, as we dwell on unending firefighting in the present, but this puts an organization at risk of being unprepared when the environment or market changes and current products or services no longer suffice.

New advances in organizational science and the practice of leadership can provide the advice necessary to define and achieve the right balance for you, your function, and your organization. That is what this book is about: Creating vital organizations.

Each day, in every business, leaders make decisions about the short term versus the long term. Decisions get made around maximizing current cash flow and profits, or reinvesting and building for the long term. But if the decisions were as easy as moving money around from budget lines A to B, there would be a lot more successful businesses. A substantial portion of business failures—from the costly to the catastrophic—can be attributed to not paying attention to the right balance between maximizing Current Performance and building Future Potential. Organizations fail not only when they go out of existence; they also fail when they are not thriving, or when they are neglecting to develop the capability to innovate to meet future needs. They fail their owners, investors, customers, employees, suppliers, and the communities in which they are located.

Disruptive technologies, globalization, emerging and evolving markets, and process innovations change so fast as to keep many organizations teetering on thin profit margins that leave little room for comfort. Survivors learn how to build and lead teams or organizations that are agile and resilient, so that they can turn quickly to pursue new opportunities and can manage bumps in the road. But organizations can do more than merely survive: They can thrive.

Clarifying what organizations do to thrive begins by separating core business pursuits into two broad categories: Current Performance and Future Potential. Some organizations are great at maximizing Current Performance—streamlining costs of production, as well as delivering time-tested products and services to known segments of the marketplace. Other organizations are supremely competent at developing Future Potential—innovating new approaches and offerings, and taking risks to create or penetrate previously unknown markets. Very few organizations, functions, or even individuals are truly good at both. Those good at both are thriving, vital organizations. They are performing today and building for tomorrow.

Saying all this is easy; making it work is hard. But one fundamental truth is that effective leadership of thriving organizations is based on clear strategies, meaningful insights, and inspired action. This book tells stories of strategy, insight, and action that are backed up with rigorous research. Collectively, these stories will create a roadmap that leaders of varying levels within an organization can utilize to maximize the performance of their organizations, their functions, or their teams.

Yes, this book is based on data, metrics, and other kinds of evidence that really matters. However, the insights gained from that data will be presented in the concise format of organizational stories. Critically, these stories are grounded in science. Decision-making traps abound, since we as humans are prone to a murky soup of heuristics, stereotypes, predispositions, and cognitive biases that make true evidence-based leadership more an exception than the norm. Common wisdom is often flawed when the environment changes so fast. How can we know what's what?

We are organizational psychologists by training, schooled in the measurement of human foibles. Importantly, our focus is not psychopathology (though it is certainly present in the workplace) or the therapy that is often imagined in a narrow definition of psychology. We are devoted to studying how people work, how teams perform, and how organizations function and thrive. Throughout this book, we will present a framework for thinking about and improving organizational effectiveness, and how to read the environment—seeing through and working around the biases we all naturally bring to the workplace—in order to both maximize Current Performance and build Future Potential. Within the private sector, organizations that are successful at achieving this balance, those that are vital, have been shown to have higher performance on a variety of metrics compared to their singularly focused counterparts. Non-profits and public sector organizations have shown similar patterns of success with their own respective measures of outcome performance.

The suggestions, advice, and anecdotes you will come across in this book are applicable not just to public or for-profit businesses, but more broadly to all types of organizations. While every organization is unique, there are clear principles that apply to a variety of organizational types because they affect the two things at the heart of these organizations: people and goals. Organizations exist when groups of people come together to accomplish things they could not accomplish on their own. The principles outlined in this book can be applied across all types of organizations and can give any of them an edge at achieving one of the most important goals out there: to be successful at whatever tasks the organization was originally formed to achieve.

Providing a point of view on organizational functioning is easy. Ensuring that any resulting guidance is grounded in science is not. There are of course many pundits who do not hesitate to offer advice. Later chapters will highlight how to critically evaluate strategy and performance, and resist the gravitational pull of the human biases and heuristics that may have their origins in useful shortcuts, but can often lead us astray. For instance, how many times have you heard the phrase "people join organizations but leave bosses"? But try this the next time you have a large group together. Ask for a show of hands as to how many people left their last job because of their boss. In a room of 30 or 40 people, only 10–20% may agree. In general, the relationship with one's direct supervisor, the boss, is not the reason why most people leave organizations. In fact, bosses are almost invariably one of the most positive aspects cited about organizations in employee surveys. Are there horrible bosses out there? Yes. Are there people out there who left their last job because of their horrible boss? Yes. But the statement that "people join organizations but leave bosses" is an overgeneralization that simply does not hold true for the vast majority.

One key to figuring out what is real and what is based on faulty assumptions—and to helping people build or lead an organization—is knowing which questions to ask. Asking the right questions about the organization and its performance is critical not only to be successful, but also to maintain that position over the long term. For instance, one president of a company that was struggling with quality and performance issues posed this question to his senior management team: "What *can* we be good at?" By framing the question that way, he completely divorced his organization from a key constituency: His current customers. He was unintentionally focusing way off into the distance in a long-term view. A more important question for a struggling organization aimed at the here and now is: "What do we ***need*** to be good at?" Organizations don't exist in a vacuum: They exist to serve others, whether those others are within another part of the organization or are external to the organization. "What *can* you be" is long-term potential (exploration), while "what do you *need* to be in order to get to the long term" is short-term performance (execution). For an organization to succeed, those questions must be asked and executed on in tandem.

We have spent decades studying and assessing organizations, using metrics, dashboards, large-scale employee or customer surveys, extensive research linking various cultural (or softer) indicators to revenue or profit, as well as interviews, focus groups, and qualitative color commentary to tie it all together. We have worked with about forty of the Fortune 100 and almost ninety of the Fortune 500. We have similarly worked intimately with numerous start-ups and other smaller organizations across a wide variety of industries, including non-profits, governmental agencies, non-governmental organizations, and educational institutions. We have drawn from our extensive experience across these various industries to form the conclusions and advice presented here.

Throughout the book, we mix into our story-telling:

- Analogies (e.g., why trying to lose weight is like acting on business metrics—standing on the scale is the easy part);

- Anecdotes from organizational life (e.g., how a few calls a day from a well-known CEO drove more business improvement than all the good intentions in the world);
- Historical comparisons (e.g., what nineteenth-century Russia can teach about labor relations);
- Fundamentals of business strategy (e.g., how employee engagement is not as strategic as people think);
- Case studies (e.g., stories of how listening carefully to the highest performers—such as President's Club sales people—can be paradoxically tricky and yet easy, and hugely informative);
- Research (e.g., the psychology of and behavioral-economic findings on unjustified dependence on social norms when under stress); and
- Practice-tested tips and advice (e.g., how a small "nudge" of a few sentences can dramatically increase the usefulness of employee dialog).

Readers will learn on two levels. On an individual level, they will learn about how their decision-making is influenced or biased, unexpectedly and unknowingly, by natural human tendencies. For instance, people often think that balancing Current Performance and Future Potential is a trade-off in a zero-sum game. Yet, if instructed properly about these concepts, leaders can break out of this trap and create conditions allowing for both to occur simultaneously in an organization. And on an organizational level, they will learn how these tendencies can affect and damage decision-making. Importantly, they will learn how to overcome these influences to succeed as individuals and as leaders of teams, departments, or entire organizations.

Each chapter will introduce measures or questions that will allow you to evaluate your own organization and gauge how it stacks up on the issues covered by this book and, we hope, will provide some insights on how to address any shortcomings identified.

CHAPTER 2

What Is Vitality?

The Elephant in the Room

Cristián Samper has a big problem. His job as head of the Wildlife Conservation Society (WCS) is to preserve wildlife, not to bear witness to its extinction. But if you examine the history of humanity as it relates to protecting wildlife, you may rapidly come to the conclusion that the odds of his being successful are not in his favor. Yet, once you get to know him, and learn what the WCS is doing to prevent species extinction, you may just change your mind. The WCS mission—to preserve wildlife and wild places—will be a hard-fought battle over many years, and will be won only if the majority of us see the long-term benefit in doing so. The long-term success of WCS will be judged by how well it carries out this mission. WCS initially built its reputation by saving the American buffalo from extinction, which was a real success story, and it is now doing some extraordinary things around the globe to prevent the extinction of other species, such as elephants.

Here is what WCS is up against: In Africa today, there are approximately 35,000–40,000 elephants killed each year for their ivory, out of a total population of about 500,000. Research studies have determined that, at this rate of poaching, the population is not sustainable and that elephants will rapidly vanish from the earth.[1] Financially, the numbers are a bit staggering. An elephant's tusks are worth about $6,000 to a poacher, who typically must deliver them to shady marketplaces, full of risk, as they are dominated by

[1] Wittemyer, G. et al., "Illegal Killing for Ivory Drives Global Decline in African Elephants," Proceedings of the National Academy of Sciences, USA, 2014.

crime syndicates and terrorist organizations such as Al-Shabaab in Somalia, Lord's Resistance Army in Central Africa, and Boko Haram in Nigeria. These organizations can turn around and sell the ivory from a pair of tusks on the black market in places like China, where ivory has a long history as a luxury good and is highly prized, for over $300,000. It has been estimated that 40% of Al-Shabaab's operating budget comes from trading in poached ivory. This is a very lucrative market and important source of income for these unsavory organizations.[2] So how can WCS break the cycle?

Since 2003, in the Luangwa Valley, Zambia, and under the guidance and stewardship of WCS, the Community Markets for Conservation (COMACO),[3] has been able to create a growing population of farmers (109,322 as of December 2014) who have committed to giving up the illegal poaching of elephants and other wildlife. In return, these farmers receive training on farming techniques and a ready market for any surplus produced, which includes peanut butter, honey, and produce. The efforts have proven so successful that their products are now sold under the brand name "It's Wild," and can be found at some of the stores of the corporate supporters of the program, such as the retail chain Shop-Rite and the South African grocery store Pick n Pay.

The result? Since inception, farmers' incomes have tripled and food-crop variety has increased by 40%. Farmers who had previously struggled to produce enough food to see them through to the next harvest are now using the increased income to send their children to school—creating a better future for them and otherwise providing for their families. And the wildlife? An estimated 1400 illegal hunters, who annually killed 5000 wild animals, including elephants and hippopotamuses, have given up poaching as their livelihood—and that's just in the one valley.[4] The Vitality of the wildlife in this valley, which was in decline, has begun to increase, and the illegal poaching has mostly ceased. People's short-term orientation of poaching in order just barely to make ends meet has slowly been shifted to one where they can prosper in the here-and-now, but also see longer term futures for themselves

[2] "The Tragic Price of Ivory," *The Week*, March 15, 2014.
[3] Community Markets for Conservation, 2014.
[4] Messenger, S., "Exclusive Interview with an Elephant Poacher," *The Doto*, January, 2014, and Lewis, D. "Feeding Conservation: An African Vision for Restoring Biodiversity," *National Geographic*, Posted by Wildlife Conservation Society, December 18, 2014.

and their children. Achieving this short-term versus long-term balance, what we will call Vitality, has been effective. The farmers are prospering and wildlife is recovering.

The Nuts and Bolts of Manufacturing

What does the illegal poaching of elephants have to do with your business? Plenty. The challenge faced by WCS mirrors those faced by other organizations; namely, that any organization must focus on future possibilities while also maintaining a current business practice.

Consider an example a little closer to home involving a manufacturer of electrical components. This company faced a basic dilemma: How to optimize efficiency while building new production capabilities at the same time. The production executive needed to increase speed while reducing costs and waste. Simultaneously, the heads of research and development (R&D) and product design needed to experiment with new features, which risked unpredictable quality issues and definitely decreased efficiency. If that wasn't enough, the head of marketing kept asking to change up the production lines in order to provide what amounted to blue or red versions of their core products. This is the classic Vitality challenge.

Vitality exists when the appropriate balance is created between the execution of current revenue streams—creating the cash-flow needed to allow an organization to operate—along with the simultaneous exploration of future revenue-stream potentials, including the development of new products, services, and markets that will keep the business competitive and relevant in the long term. In this case, the manufacturer followed the practices of Vitality, along with the supporting pillars of agility and resiliency, in how it eventually came to manage its product lifecycles. In simplified form, each product that this manufacturer produced was tracked by years since the last "refresh." The company conducted research on the expected lifecycle of its products, or how long each product was viable if left unchanged in the marketplace. Confirming a product life span of five years, they then determined that each year 20% of their product catalog would need to be refreshed, either by being given new capabilities or being completely redesigned to be current for the marketplace. Every five-year period would therefore see a complete turnover of their product line to new and enhanced products. There is a certain predictability to this. In order to achieve 20% ratio of new or enhanced products each year, a certain amount needed to be set aside for R&D and other efforts to innovate. They knew how many people in engineering, marketing, production, and so forth were needed, and on which products they should be focused. They tracked the progress they made towards achieving their 20% per year refresh targets and their longer-term five-year product-line turnover target. They considered themselves scoring well on Vitality if they were on track to make their targets. When they fell short, they could drill in and see why a product redesign was falling behind schedule and, what was needed to be done to get back to their Vitality targets.

The Harvest Waits for No One

Have you ever lain awake at night wondering how best to harvest the fruit of the jatropha plant? It is a pretty safe bet to say that most people have not given it much thought. But one person who has is Gary Stich, the CEO of Oxbo Corporation. Oxbo, a manufacturer of specialty harvesting equipment, states its mission as to "Provide innovative solutions to agribusiness worldwide." In 2007 Goldman Sachs labeled Jatropha fruit, which has very oily seeds, as one of the best candidates for biofuel production. But there was no easy way to mechanically harvest the crop at scale. To appropriately harvest it, you have to pick only the ripe fruit from this small bushy plant, which can grow in marginal conditions, maximizing the oil content contained in the seeds. And you need to do this without damaging the plant itself, so that other fruit can continue to ripen and be picked at the appropriate time. Fast forward to 2015. After field-testing several harvester models, it turns out the Oxbo 9240 Jatropha Harvester, based on Oxbo's coffee harvester, does all that just about perfectly.

Year in and year out, Oxbo must strike a balance between Current Performance and Future Potential. Its business cycles are not based on fiscal years or calendar years but on harvests. In the northern hemisphere, things start to get busy in August, and by September things are positively roaring. This is the season of performance—when the company must execute at maximum capacity and efficiency. Many of the specialty harvesters that Oxbo makes are the size of small houses and cost hundreds of thousands of dollars. To make optimal use of these assets, they are often run continuously during the harvest. A farmer cannot afford to have a major piece of machinery sitting in a field not working, putting the annual crop in jeopardy.

If a harvester has a mechanical issue during the harvest period, Oxbo is on it. Middle of the night? Rain pouring down? They are there. During this intense period of activity, it would be very easy to say that the company has no time to pay attention to anything but the harvest itself. However, Oxbo has chosen a different path. Stich knows that Current Performance must be maintained, and at the same time you must pay attention to building the Future Potential of the company. That Future Potential may be related to annual business and strategy processes, or it may be related to refining the next generation of harvester, or inventing a new harvester for a potential up-and-coming crop like Jatropha. For instance, Oxbo performs an annual employee survey. It would be easy to push off this process into less busy times, but Oxbo always conducts it during this hectic period. Very simply, if you can achieve the benchmarks and goals suggested by your strategy and set forth in your employee survey during this period of maximum Current Performance, you can be pretty sure that you are doing okay during the rest of the year as well. There is of course a structural separation between those focusing on the mechanics of the survey and those focusing on the mechanics of the harvesters, but Oxbo has consistently achieved high response rates on the survey among all employees. This is but one example of how they push ahead during times of peak performance with their future planning efforts.

Vitality Balance

The stories above highlight three organizations' approaches to balancing Current Performance with Future Potential. Each illustrates an important point about Vitality: It is simultaneous. While it may be tough, and met with resistance, the Vitality process of balancing the here-and-now with the future is never an either/or choice. They both must happen at the same time. For short stretches, organizations can emphasize one over the other. On the one hand, start-up companies, business units, or "new-venture" functions can work on developing the future, so long as they remain funded without having to generate their own cash in the short term. On the other hand, organizations in relatively stable environments can push hard within appropriate windows of time to drive production or revenue. But these are temporary situations. Start-ups will eventually run out of funding, and organizations who delay innovation risk stagnation.

Figure 2.1 illustrates the balance that must be struck. On the vertical axis we have Future Potential and on the horizontal axis Current Performance.

Your organization is in the upper left-hand box if you see yourself as focused on creating Future Potential, but not generating what is needed to keep the organization running as it currently exists. The work done here is risky, such as investments in developing products or services with an unproven return. Many start-ups fall in here, and they cope with the lack of Current Performance by bringing in venture capital or other investment to carry them to the point where their Future Potential begins to become Current Performance. New-venture groups within larger organizations also fall here, where their efforts are funded by more mature product lines.

As start-ups get traction in the marketplace, and as new ventures become established products, what was once Future Potential begins to pay dividends in Current Performance As these markets mature, initially high margins become narrower, as competitive differentiation is less about unique or innovative design, and more about speed, reliability, and eventually lower cost. Delivery becomes standardized and streamlined, enabling greater mass production. At this point, the balance has swung to maximizing Current Performance, which places you in the lower right-hand box. Eventually, products risk becoming price-sensitive commodities. Say you have to stop on the

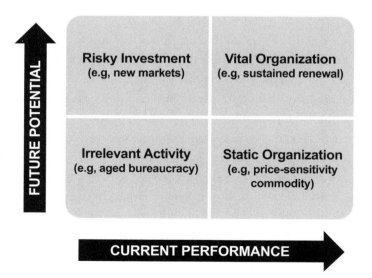

Fig. 2.1   The Vitality Matrix

way home from work to fill up the tank with gas. If there are two gas station next to each other, and one is selling a gallon of gas substantially more cheaply than the other, assuming everything else is equal, you will go for the cheaper gas. (Major gasoline brands work very hard and mostly unsuccessfully to differentiate themselves from the competition.)

If you are unfortunate enough to be part of an organization whose products or services are performing poorly in both the realms of Current Performance and Future Potential, you are in the lower left-hand box, and your organization is engaged in what can only be called irrelevant activity. These are organizations that may have had an attractive product at one point—say a record store—but because they neglected or did not clearly see the future, they simply could not compete when a disruptive technology or other environmental change came along.

The ultimate goal of appropriately balancing Current Performance with Future Potential is to be placed securely in the upper right-hand cell. Here is where your Current Performance is creating a healthy organization, which continually renews itself so to stay current with its products and services amid changing market or other environmental conditions. How you define your balance, as well as nurture and monitor it, is the task of building and leading a vital organization.

Commonality of Vitality

WCS, Oxbo, and the electrical component manufacturer are stories of Vitality—creating, managing, and leading a vital organization through the proper balance of short- and long-term needs, and building the resiliency and agility to enable that to happen gracefully. While the activities and characteristics that would define success in the three examples were very different, their overall goals were in fact very similar. They were all making sure that the performance of their respective organizations was focused not only on the here-and-now, but also on long-term success.

A vital organization is one that successfully balances the maximization of Current Performance with the development of Future Potential, and is supported by the characteristics of resiliency (the ability to bounce back from adversity and consistently risie to face challenges), as well as agility (the ability to get things done quickly, to try new things, and to "fail fast"). In academic circles, this is similar to "Organizational Ambidexterity," the simultaneous pursuit and balance of execution (Current Performance) alongside exploration (Future Potential).

More than ever, organizations struggle with tensions driven by the need to optimize Current Performance—to make money now—while building capacity for the future—to invest in potential. Competition in the global marketplace is fierce, and the demand for immediate return on investment is intense. Wall Street brutally punishes companies that miss their target numbers. When IBM announced fourth quarter 2014 earnings that Wall Street did not like, even though it beat analysts' estimates, its stock lost over 2% of its value—$3.45 per share—in just one day. At the same time, products, companies, and even industries can become obsolete faster than ever. The demise of the drive-in theater shifted an industry, but it took place over the course of quite a few years. Today, things change much more quickly. It wasn't long after the introduction of cellphones that payphones began disappearing at a very rapid rate. When is the last time you actually saw a payphone? Consider the life span of the original "dumb" flip cellphone: Rather than a generation or two, it lasted only a few years before giving way to smartphones. Think back to the prevalence of book stores only a decade or so ago. Today, when you drive through a small town that still has a book store, you get warm memories and a feeling of quaintness.

At the same time, there is an inherent tension between these two forces. The more streamlined, cost-optimized, and waste-proof production processes are, for example, the harder it is to adapt to new products. Optimizing Current Performance often depends on standards, processes, and conformity in order to lock down the process and tirelessly eliminate deviations from that process, which is the mantra of Six-Sigma quality control. Building Future Potential requires investments in creativity, innovation, and working in new paradigms: in other words, shaking things up. The most successful organizations have mastered Vitality—the balance between these two.

Vitality creates the capacity to thrive in varied environments, to excel where others struggle, and to create a purposeful existence that excels, both today and tomorrow. Such organizations strike the correct balance between maximizing internal efficiencies and generating the continual change that allows them to adapt quickly and gracefully to evolving and varied external conditions (e.g., market, economic situation, competition).

The Benefits of Creating a Vital Organization

The odds are against you. And we are not talking about a weekend trip to Las Vegas or the likelihood of the Chicago Cubs winning the World Series. The competition out there is fierce and getting fiercer. Borders, Saab, Amoco, Pan Am, Blockbuster, Lehman, Woolworth's, Circuit City, Joseph Schlitz Brewing, MCI, Virgin Records.... The list of well-established, well-known brands that have disappeared is long. Remember how successful Hummer seemed to be? It became so unpopular that its parent company General Motors (GM) couldn't even sell it. And GM itself, one of the most iconic brands in the USA, as well as a host of financial-services companies, would also be on that list if not for being bailed out by the government. One research study done in 2011 found that less than one-tenth of 1% of all organizations make it to their 40th anniversary.[5] Among young companies, roughly half fail within four years, 70% by year 10. Of the organizations that failed, it was estimated that about one-third was due to either a lack of managerial experience or to the lack of balance between the maximization of Current Performance while positioning and reinventing itself for the future. The landscape and market conditions that organizations must pay attention to are increasingly complex and move with a speed that is increasingly swift. Disruptive technologies, while rapidly enhancing the ability for some organizations to compete, makes others who cannot adapt rapidly obsolete.

Apple released the first iPhone in June 2007. Since then, according to a predictable rhythm, each year has seen a new model released. Nine versions of iPhones have been created since their launch, and some analysts say Apple will have sold one billion iPhones by summer 2016. In just the last quarter of 2014, Apple sold 74 million of its newest models of the iPhone 6, helping it to post the largest quarterly corporate profit in history. This ability to maximize performance by generating sales that result in cash and profits due to the brisk sales of iPhones, while at the same time keeping up the speed of innovation and consistently coming out with new products that the consumer wants, is in no small part what has propelled Apple to become one of the most valuable publically traded companies in the world. Apple is squarely in our upper right-hand quadrant of being a vital organization.

---

[5] Hendrickson, V., "The Traits And Behaviors Of Ambidextrous Individuals: How Exploration And Exploitation Are Integrated At The Individual Level," 2015.

Over the last 20 years, there has been an ongoing search for practical and research-based guidance for how organizations can resolve the paradox of running lean and creating maximum returns with the need to innovate and consistently drive towards future capabilities. These efforts are beginning to bear fruit. Research has shown that, compared to average organizations, those that measurably exhibit more Vitality characteristics have also been shown to have higher sales growth, higher sales revenue, higher customer satisfaction, more product innovations per year, and longer survival rates.

Assessment: Evaluating your Vitality

The following questions will help you assess your current Vitality-oriented policies and procedures, and help you frame your own thinking as you read the rest of this book. For each of the statements below, check the items that reflect the reality of your organization:

- We excel on Current Performance metrics dealing with efficiencies like speed, efficiency production, service ratings, cash flow, and profitability.
- We have a healthy Future Potential "pipeline" of products and services we are experimenting with or have under development that will keep us relevant, competitive, and unique in the future.
- More than 50% of my organization's products or services have been refreshed or introduced in the last five years.
- My organization is able to balance gracefully the competing needs of executing and streamlining Current Performance, while simultaneously exploring and building Future Potential.
- We effectively share resources across the organization from successful Current Performance in order to fund efforts to build Future Potential.
- Over time, we effectively convert Future Potential ideas and innovations into streamlined execution that delivers Current Performance.
- Our company has demonstrated the ability to grow without sacrificing the quality of what we deliver.
- I have confidence in the future of my organization.

Give yourself one point for each statement that you could clearly and unhesitatingly check. If you checked seven or eight items, then your Vitality discipline is better than most, and you will be well-positioned to leverage even the more advanced concepts in this book. If you checked five or six items, you have a pretty good grounding, and would benefit from refining some of your weak points. If you checked four or fewer items, you likely struggle with finding the balance between Current Performance and Future Potential. This book should help you identify and articulate some clear needs to improve the performance of your organization.

Whatever your score, these statements and questions should help you frame your own needs as you explore the rest of this book for ideas and tips that will help you streamline your own Current Performance while simultaneously building Future Potential.

To take this and other assessments online, and get an interactive, customized report, visit OV-CVO.com.

CHAPTER 3

Strategy

Creating a Successful Strategy

Company X, a middle-market retailer of soft goods, was struggling. Revenues were declining. Management considered expanding their store footprints, but were hesitant, given the company's sliding revenues. There was no clear brand identity making them stand out in a crowded market. While the company managed to sell a great deal of merchandise, sales were often at an unprofitable clearance price; this was especially dangerous for a business with such a low profit margin. The CEO changed course in an attempt to revive the company: The retailer would provide the fashion and quality of a well-established department store (like Macy's or JC Penny's) at the price points of big-box discount stores such as Target or Wal-Mart. This vision excited and energized employees, who were inspired to try and make it work. But would the CEO succeed, keep the failing company sputtering along, or possibly hasten its decline?

Before the fate of Company X is revealed, it is important to talk about what makes a good strategy. Stop and think about what the word "strategy" means. Can you define it? For most people, it has a hazy definition that involves being connected to a bigger picture or a broad plan. The actual definition, according to Webster's dictionary, is more specific. Strategic is defined as being "of great importance within an integrated whole or to a planned effect." Defining and implementing an effective strategy is key to achieving

Vitality—the right balance between your Current Performance and Future Potential.

For your business to formulate and execute a successful strategy, you need to go beyond both the common and dictionary definitions of the word. We prefer the more precise and effective description offered by Michael Porter, professor at the Institute for Strategy and Competitiveness at the Harvard Business School: Strategy is "the creation of a unique and valuable position."[1] Strategically successful companies base their plans on this premise. So how do you create your own unique and valuable position? Start by addressing these core questions:

- What can you do better than anyone else?
- What can you do to make it easier to earn and maintain the respect, repeat business, and, ultimately, the money of customers?
- If you work in a for-profit organization, how can you make your work unique and harder for your competitors to copy?

Once you've identified ways to make your company stand out, it's time to craft a specific strategy to reach that goal. We're going to look at key characteristics of effective strategies, but first, let's look at a few things that often get mistaken for strategy: Goals, ambitions, and operational effectiveness.

Goals and Ambition

Aspirational statements may make employers and employees feel good, but that's all they do. Saying things like "we will be #1 in our market," or "we will be a $1 billion dollar company within 10 years" imply a destination, but do nothing to help you get there. These may be fine ambitions, and they may help frame a vision of the future. Employees might find them motivating (although never as much as executives expect). However, they are not strategies, because they say nothing about the specific steps that the organization must take to achieve the ambition.

---

[1] Porter, M., "What is Strategy," *Harvard Business Review*, 1996, 68. Further citations of this work are given in the text.

Operational Effectiveness

An operationally effective company is one that executes its core business processes well. For your particular company, your focus might be to reduce costs, increase speed, reduce waste or errors, maximize conformity, or streamline other aspects of production or service delivery. At some point, it is very likely your own organization has floated around mantras like "Do more with less" or "Give 110 percent." All of these focus on efficient resource management—getting more output for the same or reduced input. Ultimately, these efforts are all about cost control. However, you cannot cost-cut your way to success. Operational efficiencies are about delivering greater efficiency, lower per-unit costs, and performing activities that are similar to your competitors, but doing them better. Operational efficiencies are critical to overall organizational success, but they are not strategic.

So, what is "strategic"? Formulating and executing a strategy is about developing organizational capabilities and choosing how to deploy them. They are all focused on things like delivering greater value, establishing the ability to charge more than competitors, and performing different activities than competitors (or similar activities in different ways). Here are the three traits of an effective strategy:

Customizing Unique Strategies

Focusing on and implementing different activities than your competition is all about making your organization unique. What if Wal-Mart tried to be successful in exactly the same way as Target? The two companies are similar, but have slight differences in retail locations and customer base. Imagine if instead they chased the same customers, merchandising, pricing, geographies, or logistics? If they were equally successful, there would be no reason for a customer to prefer one retailer to the other, making success essentially random. Instead of duplicating other organizations, sustained strategies capitalize on factors competitors find costly, time-consuming, or impossible to copy. Even non-competitive organizations need strategies that are uniquely tailored to their organization's strengths, so that leaders can make decisions with more efficiency, effectiveness, or impact. This means that good strategies will not look like others in the marketplace.

Just as you cannot cost-cut your way to success, you cannot copy your way to competitive differentiation. Pursue all the best practices, industry benchmarks, or standard operating procedures you want. While these can help you become more efficient, they cannot help you deliver greater, unique value to your customers.

Of course, differentiation isn't enough to succeed. As Porter reminds us, being unique does not necessarily lead to a competitive edge. Different doesn't always mean better, especially where customers are concerned. It is, however, a prerequisite to success. Competitiveness is creating a differentiation, a uniqueness, which is valued in the eyes of your customers.

Framework for Action

Strategies guide business leaders by suggesting which paths should be pursued. Effective strategies directly address specific challenges and bottlenecks. They suggest *how* you will achieve that target. Clearly communicated strategies help managers within the organization make decisions that are aligned with the strategy, and allow the members of the organization all to move in the same direction.

Strategies inform the direction an organization should take. For example, a company may need to decide between doubling down on expanding current client relationships or expanding into new markets. Those priorities are accompanied by investments to head down either path. Organizational leaders are responsible for making choices: You cannot go in two different directions at the same time. A clear strategy helps inform your decisions so you choose the best path to take.

Explore New Territory

Developing an identity that makes your organization unique is difficult enough. *Staying* unique is an even bigger challenge. Your competition will try to copy you, rendering your uniqueness not so special anymore, or they will emphasize their own differences. Technologies, global markets, resource costs, or customer needs can all change rapidly. The wildly innovative and in-demand products of yesterday quickly become the price-sensitive commodities of today. To remain relevant, organizations need to continually improve not just how they create value, but improve the competence with how they find new ways to create value. This is the only way uniqueness can be sustained.

Setting Course Without Strategy

Back to the fate of Company X: Its strategy was to provide the fashion and quality of a department store at the price points of the big-box discounters. Now that you understand the key characteristics of an effective strategy, it's clear that this plan was not, in fact, a real strategy. It was an ambition that did not direct any unique efforts to deliver customer value. Everyone wants to offer better products or services at a lower price than the competition. That ambition was not helpful in articulating how the organization should be successful or how it would compete. Without a clear strategy, the changes that the company made—most notably, an overhaul of inventory-management systems to provide the styles, sizes, and colors to match the weekly advertisements of loss-leaders that drove store traffic, as well as an expansion plan into new geographies—were not enough. Company X could not capitalize on strengths and assets that competitors could not copy. Company X limped along for the subsequent decade, trying to find the right way to compete. Eventually, it declared bankruptcy, liquidated all assets, and closed all its stores.

Chasing Rainbows

Market Dominance, Most Innovative Products, Best Customer Service, Most Attractive Stores, Lowest Price…you get the idea. All of these great-sounding phrases are lofty goals—but they are not strategies, or even a path to strategic success. Strategy involves crafting a step-by-step plan that details exactly how you will attempt to achieve market dominance, or how you will provide the best customer service. Goals are less connected to the business, have little to no motivational impact on the troops in the trenches, and do not suggest a specific course of action regarding how to achieve that goal.

Some companies may use ambiguous goals as substitutes for strategies because they don't have any concrete actionable plans. For employees to be motivated, more is needed than the simply lofty goal-phrases put out by some corporate leaders, who then wonder why the rank and file don't get just as excited about them as they do.

Here is the reason: No one has ever seen someone else's rainbow. Rainbows have no physical manifestation; you can't physically feel them. They cast no shadows and have no refection. They are completely ephemeral. Rainbows are so moving that many cultures around the world have developed legends about them. For instance, each time the medieval Germans saw a rainbow, they believed that the world would last another 40 years. Some North American Indians refer to the rainbow as a pathway of souls. In Ireland, of course, rainbows were believed to bring good luck, leading to a pot of gold. All of these interpretations—however mythical, lofty, romantic, or desirable they may be—were based on a fundamental lack of understanding of what a rainbow is.

A rainbow is created when a beam of light passes through water droplets, is diffracted, and shines on the color receptors in your eye. Rainbows are a creation of the physical properties that exist between the light, the water, your eye, and your brain. They exist only because you are there looking at them. Different people see different rainbows, or different light beams passing through different water droplets reflecting uniquely off of the color receptors in their eyes. Rainbows may appear very similar, but each of us perceives the rainbow in a unique way.

Organizations are constantly looking for their own rainbows—or perhaps more accurately, the pot of gold at the end of the rainbow. They create all sorts of messaging to motivate employees to see the same rainbow that the leader at the top of the organization sees. But just as people see rainbows in a unique way, each employee needs to internalize organizational goals in their own fashion. They need to understand their role in the organization's strategy in order to help achieve its goals. Each person in the organization, including those working on Current Performance, as well as those building Future Potential, has a role to play, whether it is the person working the assembly line, the analyst assessing company options, or the head of treasury managing the company's funds. Each has a part to play in the ultimate success of the organization, and part of management's job is to make the explicit connection between the various roles in the organization and how they will enable the strategy. This becomes especially difficult if the strategy isn't communicated throughout the organization from the upper levels of management.

In one company, for instance, the CEO communicated his vision of being a billion-dollar-a-year company. Other than for a very few senior managers, that vision meant nothing to employees. Their jobs wouldn't change if that goal was realized, other than they might have to do more work. A vision needs to be motivational and must provide a rationale for the employee as to why he or she joined and stays with the organization.

With the right vision or goals, employees will likely be more effective in their work, because most people want to feel as though their work is meaningful in some way. However, just as individuals have a unique vision of personal rainbows, they also have a unique vision of why they work to achieve the organization's goals. This is true despite commonalities that exist regarding what people want out of the work environment. Humans are similar beings, and in building a culture the organization and its managers must recognize and celebrate both that uniqueness and those similarities.

Strategy and Vitality

In addition to a clearly articulated strategy, successful companies have another thing in common: Vitality. In order to achieve Vitality within your organization, you need to strike the right balance between Current Performance and Future Potential. That's no easy task, but it is the essence of being successful both today *and* tomorrow. Strategic positioning has a complementary aim, rooted in leveraging the unique value-contributions of an organization, or even a specific division or work group. The rest of this chapter blends these concepts into a model of organizational effectiveness that helps to focus the attention of leaders and formulation of strategy. We call this the Vitality Model.

Within the framework of Vitality, a strategy must help articulate how to improve Current Performance while simultaneously directing investments for Future Potential. It shows how an organization performs now *and* in the future. It guides decisions, both at the top of the organization, as well as on the ground. While each organization's approach to becoming more vital must be unique, there is a starting framework that can be used to articulate strategy.

What are the fundamental areas that organizations attempt to change, whether Current Performance or Future Potential? What are the most common challenges companies face? To address these questions, many different models of organizational effectiveness exist,[2] ranging from the very simple to more complex, academic, or even hybrid approaches. Stepping back from any single model, there are six enduring challenges that every organization faces in its pursuit of growth and financial sustainability. Each of these challenges

[2] Collins, J., "Five Stages of Organizational Decline" in *How The Mighty Fall,* 2009; Burke-Litwin Model in Burke, W., and Litwin, G., "A Casual Model of Organizational Performance and Change," *Journal of Management,* vol. 18, no 3, 1992; Open Systems Model in Katz, D., and Kahn, R., *The Social Psychology of Organizations,* 1978; The Balanced Scorecard in Kaplan, R., and Norton, D., *Translating Strategy into Action: The Balanced Scorecard,* 1996; McKinsey 7 S Framework in Peters, T., and Waterman, R., *In search of excellence: Lessons from America's best-run companies,* 1982; The High Performance Model in Wiley, J.W., and Brooks, S.M., "The high performance organizational climate: How workers describe top performing units." In N. S. Ashkanasy, C. Wilderom, & M. F. Peterson (Eds.), *The Handbook of Organizational Culture and Climate,* 2000.

embodies the tension of Vitality—choices to focus the control of maximizing Current Performance while enabling the creativity to build Future Potential. These tensions define the challenges that face organizations today.

The Six Challenges of Vitality

1. **Leadership.** Sound leadership is about both driving current execution while creating and communicating a vision that defines the future. Vital organizations balance a leadership culture of "making the numbers" with the ability to nurture new leadership and new directions.

2. **Employees.** Effective organizations are able to create a talented and engaged workforce where employees can thrive. Vital organizations develop and nurture organizational competencies, which are the knowledge and skills of the workforce working in tandem with the organization to adapt to meet changing challenges. This instills confidence in employees, in terms both of the organization as a whole as well as their own personal well-being.

3. **Processes.** The work of an organization is defined by its processes. Having efficient and innovative processes is critical. There is an inherent tension between maximizing efficiency while cultivating the flexibility that embraces innovation—quality control and standards versus customization and adaptability.

4. **Offerings.** Committing to a brand, a product catalog with attractive offerings, or a set of defining services helps an organization be successful by creating value for today's customers. But the more fixed an organization is on specific offerings, the harder it is to respond to new marketplace opportunities or threats.

5. **Service.** An exceptional-service orientation is often the key differentiator between two organizations with similar products, capabilities, and footprints. Customer loyalty is achieved by a consistent experience. Similar to production processes, however, the more consistent and locked-down an organization's service engine is, the harder it is to adapt to new customer needs or emergent marketplace forces.

6. **Customers.** Current loyal customers are the engine of any organization's performance. Growth, however, is dependent on cultivating new customers and new marketplace segments without unduly sacrificing existing ones. Vital organizations develop the ambidexterity to manage both.

These six challenges are depicted in the Vitality Model (see Fig. 3.1). Both Current Performance execution and Future Potential explorations run through and interact with each of these six key challenge areas, represented here as circles. Current Performance and Future Potential stretch and reach to the other, always balanced—not equally, but as befits your organization—and co-dependent on each other, as your Current Performance work helps fund and support Future Potential efforts, which in turn cycle back into Current Performance.

While there are enduring challenges within each of these six key areas—the circles on the model—often the toughest struggles organizations face deal with managing the tensions *across* these areas. For example:

- Processes maximized for Current Performance are at odds with developing innovative offerings. The most optimized production lines are less flexible to adapt to new products.

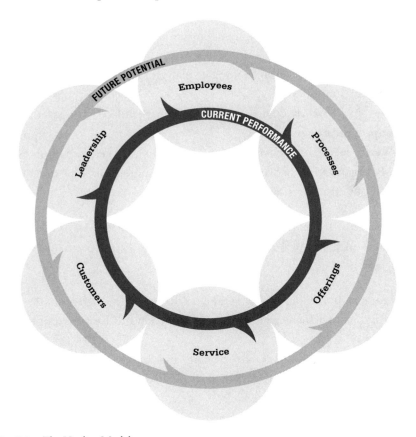

Fig. 3.1 The Vitality Model

- Service paradigms that are currently effective for delivering products to current customer segments may not be optimal for chasing new customer segments. What worked well for US-based customers may not work for those in China. Service systems set up to support face-to-face customer interactions would need an overhaul to support online transactions.
- Upgrading organizational competencies with new kinds of employee talent can sacrifice process and production efficiencies, and may make current employees uncertain about their own futures. For example, the acquisition of a new business-to-business consulting group can demand new processes to realize this new potential.

Assessment: Defining Strategic Targets

To help you address the core questions from this chapter, read each of the statements below, and check the items that reflect the reality of your organization:

- Our strategy is unique to my organization, and is clearly different from our competitors.
- Our strategy offers clear, actionable plans for improvement and steps for implementation.
- We are aware of environmental and marketplace changes that will impact the organization
- We are successfully navigating environmental/marketplace changes.
- My organization or work group generates unique products or services that our customers cannot obtain elsewhere.

Compared to the competition (or our customers' alternatives), we have clear advantages in <u>Current Performance</u>—what it takes to execute—in the following areas:

- Leadership (Leadership is sound, with the right leaders in the right positions to achieve effective execution; it rewards execution of existing plans.)
- Employees (Employees are thriving and highly performing in their respective areas, having the necessary skill sets, training, tools, and environment for performance.)
- Processes (Internal and external procedures are efficient, innovative, high-quality, and have effective cost control.)

- Offerings (Offerings to our customers are attractive, with products and services that are currently in demand.)
- Service (Our customer-service orientation and support systems are exceptional; customers feel great when interacting with the organization.)
- Customers (Our customer base is well-defined and loyal, with high levels of cross-selling, up-selling, or repeat business.)

Compared to the competition (or our customers' alternatives), we have clear advantages in <u>Future Potential</u>—what it takes to explore and transform—in the following areas:

- Leadership (Leadership is spending time envisioning, inventing, and communicating the future; it rewards efforts to step back and develop potential.)
- Employees (The organization attracts plenty of highly talented people and can retain the best; it experiments with developing new areas of competence.)
- Processes (Internal and external procedures are agile, allowing for continuous adaptation and improvement.)
- Offerings (We have a healthy "pipeline" of new offerings the marketplace will find attractive in the future.)
- Service (We are building our brand with effective marketing, sales, and brand management; service approaches are agile in adapting to new offerings or new customer needs.)
- Customers (Our customers are brand advocates to others and are excited about any new products and services we roll out; we explore new marketplace segments.)

Vital organizations would clearly endorse all of the first five items, at least four of the Current Performance items, and have an undeniable clarity on one or two of the Future Potential items. If all of the Future Potential items were checked, it may reflect too diffuse a strategy: A clear competitive edge across all six aspects of the Vitality Model is unusual and may be unsustainable.

To take this and other assessments online, and get an interactive, customized report, visit OV-CVO.com.

CHAPTER 4

Leadership

The Relentless Commitment to the Yin and Yang of Vitality

You have crafted your strategy. You have refined your sense of the Current Performance that defines success today, as well as envisioned Future Potential that should ensure your relevance tomorrow. So now what?

The ideas and the vision need to move from inside the heads of a few, through relentless commitment by the top leadership team, to the duality of Vitality, and into implementation by the rest of your organization. But take a moment to pause and answer this question: What business, exactly, are you in?

Before you give a knee-jerk answer, consider this: Starbucks is not just about selling coffee, but about selling an experience that encourages people to linger. This allows it to sell (in addition to the 87,000 drink permutations it claims it makes) breakfast and lunch food, protein bars, water, and CDs— and that is just in the actual coffeehouses. Go into any large grocery store and you can buy Starbucks-branded coffee and even ice cream. Starbucks will not stagnate if it ever saturates the coffee market (which feels unlikely). This wider frame on its business allows for experimenting with many avenues of Future Potential.

Fujifilm has a similarly expansive frame, though born more of necessity. As early as the 1980s, Fujifilm began preparations for the coming digital-photography boom by exploring product lines other than camera film. Building from its considerable skills as a chemical company, it diversified into products such as cosmetics (with anti-oxidation properties similar to those that keep photographic film from fading) and coatings on LCD monitors (another short step from traditional film). Fujifilm weathered the digital revolution, whereas Kodak, which ignored the digital threat, did not.

Like Starbucks or Fujifilm, the definition of your organization must flow from your strategy. Consider the story of Harley Davidson, America's top-selling motorcycle company. Today, it is a $13 billion business. But it was not always that way. Back in the 1970s, this now-iconic brand struggled, losing market share to Japanese companies. The company decided that rather than competing directly with Japanese manufacturers on quality, they would focus on the retro appeal of their motorcycles. They sought new customers beyond their typical under-35 buyer, and attracted lots of middle-aged men who wanted to embrace the "bad boy" image that riding a Hog gave them. It worked: In 1987, half of Harley riders were under age 35, with a median income of $38,000, but by 2005, the median age had risen to almost 47, with a household income of $83,000. Additionally, Harley Davidson won customers who didn't even ride motorcycles, but were happy to buy their clothing, accessories, and eat at their restaurants, because of the street cred it gave them.

Like Starbucks and Fujifilm, Harley Davidson pointedly made an effort to transform its product from just an item—a motorcycle—into a lifestyle. It succeeded so well in attracting older customers that now it once again faces a similar demographic challenge, only this time it needs to target younger customers, minorities, and women. Keep an eye on this company to see how well they succeed with this new Future Potential challenge.

Building Executive Alignment

Driving Current Performance and building Future Potential will make up two separate yet intertwined facets of your strategy. In many organizations, these two areas of focus may thrive in different parts of the organization (more on this in Chap. 5). If your organization is like most, the various members of the leadership team focus on different things. You might have individuals who watch costs with an intensity that helps keep you in business. These people might focus on routines, standardization, measurable outcomes, and institutional control. Often, though not always, these people have come up through operations, manufacturing, logistics, or accounting. They provide extraordinary value in keeping things on track, in compliance, and under budget.

You might also have people who stray from convention. They focus on the "what-if" side of business, and attend more to breaking with convention and exploring new possibilities. Their purpose is to keep products and services fresh and relevant.

Critical for Vitality is this: Do these people get along? Do they understand and support each other's points of view? Perhaps more importantly, do they understand and support each other's budgets?

The needs of Current Performance and Future Potential will often be in competition. The different people or departments tasked with focusing on one area will often advocate prioritizing their work or needs over others.

This presents a delicate balancing act for a company's CEO and top leadership team members, who must accommodate these dual needs. They can do this by making Vitality a priority and demonstrating to employees that both aspects of the business are critical to the company's long-term success. Employees at all levels, from senior leaders on down, must recognize the importance of each, and intentionally decide how much time and resources each aspect needs, based upon current market conditions and the company's specific strategy. The employees who are tasked with maintaining the business model must understand that their role includes supporting those who are pursuing new, often not-yet-profitable, ventures that will, they hope, keep the business relevant. Similarly, those tasked with developing new business opportunities (and who may view their work as more exciting or creative) must appreciate that their work is only possible with the support of the team managing the profitable arm of the business. These teams are two sides of the same coin. Without both faces, the coin is worthless.

Remember Radio Corporation of America (RCA), the American electronics company that helped pioneer broadcast television? They also had a solid business manufacturing and selling actual television sets, as well as producing the vacuum tubes that were the basic component of those bulky appliances. Their success with tubes was ultimately related to their decline. Vacuum tubes were such a significant contributor to their financials that the company's leaders could not swiftly and decisively commit to emergent solid-state transistors. They were so invested in the tube business, and faced with the significant financial challenges required to transform their business, that they labored along into irrelevance, unwilling or unable to pursue new revenue streams. In other words, they were focusing only on one side of the coin.

Aligning Strategy with Vitality

Now, consider this story of a small town farmers' market: Pleasantville is a tiny village about 30 miles north of New York City. Like many suburbs, the downtown of Pleasantville was suffering from too many empty storefronts in the late 1990s. In an attempt to revitalize the downtown, the town allowed a for-profit company, Community Markets, to run a weekend farmers' market on a short length of sidewalk adjacent to the train station. This company operated multiple markets, and the formula was the same for each: Divide the outdoor market footprint into small lots and rent them to a handful of independent local farmers and similar retailers. In Pleasantville, the market consisted of roughly a dozen lots next to a parking lot. Though residents enjoyed having access to locally sourced produce, the atmosphere of the market was chaotic, and shoppers would often leave as quickly as possible.

The market operated in this fashion for many years, even as the popularity of farmers' markets soared nationally and Pleasantville's downtown shopping area came back to life. The leaders of the company were satisfied with the revenues that were generated from the rentals, and saw no reason to evolve.

In 2010, a local resident asked the mayor of Pleasantville if he could get involved with the committee overseeing the market. It turns out there was no committee. The market was run solely by the for-profit company, which paid nothing to Pleasantville, even as it profited from renting out the village's real estate, and relied on village resources. The local resident formed his own committee, and they began discussing how to improve their market. One of their first decisions was to shift the purpose of the market: Rather than focusing simply on renting spaces to local farmers, they made it their mission to bring together community members over a shared passion for good, locally grown and sourced food.

To achieve this goal, the market was moved to accommodate additional vendors and give shoppers room to browse and socialize. The area was closed to cars, creating a safe space for pedestrians. Tables and chairs were brought in for people who wanted to enjoy their food at the market. Local musicians started playing at the market each week, and volunteers offered kids' activities such as arts and crafts, puppet shows, and yoga. In short, the market evolved from a place to food shop into a Saturday morning outing where community members could spend time with their family and friends, enjoy good food, music, and activities, and also do their food shopping.

At first, the small group of local residents tried to work with the company, but their efforts to change were met with resistance. Eventually, when the company's contract expired, the village declined to renew and instead handed over leadership to the small group of volunteers. The market continued to evolve: The group figured out a way to operate inside a local school building during the winter, allowing them to expand to a year-round market. Programming expanded to include local chefs providing cooking demonstrations, health-and-wellness talks, and more community events. The market now features more than 50 vendors and has won acclaim as the best farmers' market in the county.

This story shows the power of forward-focused leadership. A leader who understands the delicate balancing act required of businesses today—the ability to concentrate on present operations while simultaneously pursuing future opportunities needed to grow and adapt the business in a rapidly changing economy—will often run the most successful companies. What "business" was the farmers' market in? It used to be in the business of distributing produce. It evolved to become a community event.

Team Discord: When Good Vitality Goes Bad

The critical question every leader must ask is this: How do the people on these two different sides of the business work together? Your goal is integration—a wholeness or unity of perspective and effort. This doesn't mean that everyone will agree all of the time. Rather, you want an environment where leaders of operations and leaders of R&D willingly share a common vision for blending Current Performance and Future Potential. They share priorities in such a way that the operations leaders embrace investing in their cohorts' R&D budgets.

A few years back, a rapidly growing new technology company was at a crossroad. By their very nature, tech companies are volatile. With every new advancement, there's the threat of obsolescence. This particular company faced that predicament: Their current technology poised them for rapid growth and a national-market penetration that would require a 50% staff increase, but they were also aware that within a few years this same technology would be outdated. The clock was ticking. The pressure to develop new forms of revenue was intense.

Unfortunately, there was a deep disconnect within the company. The department tasked with product development saw itself as the future, and discounted the importance of the department overseeing the current revenue stream. Similarly, those responsible for the current technology that was propelling the company's success believed that the company's future lay in a transformed version of the existing product. It is possible that both departments may have been right. But without a unified strategy, both departments rushed to bring new products to market without any specific focus, and none of the products met with any success. As predicted, their once-powerful technology became obsolete, and without a new strong source of revenue, the company faltered and wound up laying off 10% of its workforce.

During this time of rapid growth and then decline, few leaders actually had much optimism that they would make the changes needed to compete in the marketplace. In a healthy company, top leaders usually have an optimistic perspective. They have faith in their abilities to steer the company. As you can see in Fig. 4.1, the organization as a whole had a manic-depressive cycle regarding optimism for the future. At the same time, top leadership showed what turned out to be an artificial hope in Year Three, followed by a plummeting to depths even lower than the employees at large. Does it come as any surprise when a company that doesn't even earn the faith of its top leadership fails?

In this case, the CEO was replaced just before posting the dismal Year Four numbers in the chart, which showed quite dramatically that the company's vice presidents had a much more dismal outlook than the rest of the employees. Within six months of the CEO's replacement, the organization

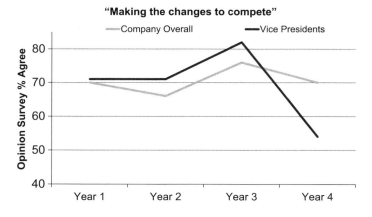

Fig. 4.1　Internal company survey

announced it would abandon three new products, including those spawned from both the innovation department as well as the largest—and aging—business unit. Two years later, the next CEO stepped down as well, amidst more aimless product development and subsequent poor earnings. Today, this company continues to struggle, and investors question whether it will survive.

Here is an example of a culture that fostered Vitality: Within a large financial services company, the top leaders—partners who owned the business—met frequently to discuss Current Performance and Future Potential. In annual business reviews, they routinely discussed how the business units that were making the most money would fund product development or market expansion of the business units that were not performing as well. The leadership team had the commitment from the heads of every department to reinvest revenue in emergent areas, because they understood the importance of balance. Just like rebalancing a retirement account, the top leaders knew that investing in new ventures, alongside managing their current portfolio, was critical to their long-term success.

The Power of Strong Leadership

Creating a culture that best manages the tension between those with operations-versus innovation-orientations happens under the leadership of a strong CEO who is able to inspire employees by proving that the company is well enough established to succeed. Oftentimes, these leaders are called Transformational CEOs: They relentlessly champion the message of Vitality, broaden and inspire others' aspirations to achieve more than they thought they could, as well as create a sense of belonging and ownership of a common vision. These CEOs are able to take the paradoxical tensions inherent in balancing the often conflicting demands of Current Performance and Future Potential. Whoever is tasked with integrating these various needs, whether it is the CEO or another member of the senior leadership team, must have a deep understanding of the needs of both Current Performance and Future Potential and how they align with the company's specific strategy in order to make the best possible decisions for the company. Imagine the Chinese yin yang symbol: Two seemingly opposite forces are actually complementary and interdependent. Each side has a dot, or a portion, in the other side to reflect the balance between the two. A strong leader understands this, and cannot only apply it to the organization, but must make it a shared vision within the company. By contrast, the top leadership team does not necessarily need to be as balanced as the CEO. As we have discussed, it's important that senior leaders share a vision of the company as a whole, are able to express dissent and consider others' ideas, and work together for the betterment of the entire organization in both the present and future. Conflict will inevitably arise as those tasked with maintaining Current Performance compete for resources with those charged with discovering Future Potential. The CEO who makes Vitality a priority will enable his or her separate department heads to function more as a team when that happens. Ultimately, a strong CEO will take decisive action when a conflict can't be resolved among senior managers.

Transformational CEOs craft a narrative for their company that promotes past and present success, while looking towards a future of relevancy and profit. The message needs to be shared throughout the entire organization in a way that feels credible to all employees, connecting the daily realities of current production to the possibilities of the organization tomorrow. Most importantly, this message needs to be practiced in all areas of the business— not just trotted out as lip service. Communicated correctly, Vitality messages will resonate with employees and inspire them.

Moving from Executive Alignment to Compelling Vision

Having a top leadership team that is relentlessly committed to Vitality— the active management of Current Performance while investing in Future Potential—is only the first step on the journey towards Vitality. The next step involves relentlessly championing your ideas for the future throughout the

The Power of the "One Thing"

In the 1991 movie *City Slickers*, Jack Palance played a weathered cowboy named Curley who gave advice to Billy Crystal's character Mitch:

Curly: Do you know what the secret of life is? [holds up his index finger] This.
Mitch: Your finger?
Curly: One thing. Just one thing. You stick to that and the rest don't mean s***.
Mitch: But, what is the "one thing"?
Curly: That's what you have to find out.

While Curley was talking about life from a personal perspective, the advice applies to business. And this "one thing" (often expanded to the "critical few") clearly varies. How might the "one thing" play out in an organization?

In the late 1980s, Alcoa's new CEO, Paul O'Neill, set his company's "one thing" as safety. The company was struggling with product lines that were not doing well and a response was needed. Investors were hoping for a focus on margins and market share, but instead O'Neill made a very public commitment to worker safety. Even though Alcoa's safety record was better than the average company in manufacturing, he wanted better. During the emphasis-on-safety announcement, when one investor asked about inventories, Mr. O'Neill's response, as documented in Charles DuHigg's *The Power of Habit*, was, "I'm not certain you heard me.... If you want to understand how Alcoa is doing, you need to look at our workplace safety figures."

While investors were skeptical and his senior management required much persuasion, the outcome spoke volumes: Lost worker-days per injury went from 1.86 to an astounding 0.2. O'Neill's cultural legacy at Alcoa continued, and the company in 2012 recorded 0.125 lost days per injury. What about company financial performance? Within one year of the emphasis on safety, company profits hit a record high. O'Neill explained to DuHigg, ""I knew I had to transform Alcoa. But you can't order people to change. So I decided I was going to start by focusing on one thing. If I could start disrupting the habits around one thing, it would spread throughout the entire company." The focus on safety caused the company to re-examine processes and products in order to achieve the safety goal. With better processes, product quality increased, along with customer satisfaction and demand for their products. In other words, Paul O'Neill's focus on and vision for Future Potential led to an improved Current Performance.

rest of the organization. Simply stating your plans is insufficient within most organizations: Saying something even in a logical way means little in terms of organizational functioning. Keeping people aligned to your vision is an ever-present effort to enlist both the hearts and minds of employees. In the end, it is all about compelling storytelling.

Consider the following example: Two financial-services organizations were ready to merge. On paper, they were an ideal match, yet they had to reconcile independent 100-year histories. The merger involved the traditional struggles to work through a cultural shift, involving restructuring, "lean" inspired cost-cutting, and redefinitions of their target markets. Reasonably, the leadership wanted to clearly communicate the new vision driving all these changes in order to give employees confidence in the company and its future, and to help them see their way through the short-term chaos of integrating the two organizations. So, through some excellent work involving both the leadership team and corporate communications, a very well-written 20-page document was drafted that articulated the need to change, the new directions, and the key values upon which the executives made their decisions. This document was exceptionally well-produced in hard copy—colors, card stock, and pictures of smiling and diverse groups of people—everything you would expect from a highly professional organization.

Except virtually no one read it. Those employees who did felt it was over-produced and typical "executive speak," providing no real useful information or having anything to do with the day-to-day realities faced by most employees. These employees were concerned about concrete issues, including the centralization of service delivery, which involved closing branches and severing customer relationships that had often stretched over more than a decade, as well as the reduction in the variety of products and services offered, which took away choices that many customers had typically valued. Furthermore, employees felt that the leadership was refocusing on some customers to the exclusion of others with longer-term relationships. Yet none of this was addressed by the glossy brochure.

This scenario sounds so familiar to many people, that many assume this example was drawn from their own organization. So what happened?

One particular executive realized that the brochure had completely missed the mark. He understood that the very polished document did not alleviate employees' concerns. Instead, he started by listening to the employee concerns mentioned above—the day-to-day frustrations that stemmed from centralizing service delivery, consolidating the product portfolio, and focusing on core customers. He took up the challenge to connect employees' concerns with how these changes were designed in order to streamline operations, increase fiscal responsibility, reduce risk, and honor customers' long-term financial needs, all in a unified effort to ensure the company's future. Ultimately, the company summed up its plans with the saying, "We are here for the ages." This communicated to employees that all the changes being made, no matter how jarring at first, served the larger goal of long-term survival. This reframing of employees' frustrations as short-term chaos did not erase all problems overnight, but it created a better dialogue, and increased both trust in leadership and more engagement among employees. The overarching lesson embodied in this example is that leadership credibility is built from messages that resonate with employees' day-to-day experiences. Decisions must make sense, without a fancy corporate communications statement, and without leaders being in the room to explain.

Assessment: Evaluating Your Leadership Team

To better answer the leadership-related questions posed by this chapter, complete the assessment below by checking all items that reflect the reality of your organization:

- ○ There is a relentless commitment across the leadership team to a vision of Vitality—a balance of streamlining Current Performance and investing in Future Potential.
- ○ There is a clear understanding of which leaders and groups are focused on Current Performance and which ones are focused on Future Potential.
- ○ There is a widely-held confidence in the future of the group and its ability to achieve its vision.
- ○ Leadership-team members are willing to consider, discuss, and implement opposing views; they have general respect for other's opinions.
- ○ Rewards and reinforcements encourage team members to look beyond their unit and work toward both the short- and long-term good of the entire organization. (This can reduce interpersonal competition and facilitate negotiations of budgets and other precious resources.)
- ○ All top leaders speak with "one voice" about the balance of short-term and long-term needs.
- ○ Communications about strategy and overall direction enable those several layers down from the top to set priorities, investing time and resources in efforts aligned with both success today and a thriving tomorrow.

All seven of these items would be present within a vital organization. If you can only check five or six items, then your priorities for improvement are clear. If you checked fewer than five items, your leadership team needs meaningful calibration as your first step in developing Vitality.

To take this and other assessments online, and get an interactive, customized report, visit OV-CVO.com.

CHAPTER 5

Developing Vital Individuals

Exploring New Domains

A German-born tailor traveled to San Francisco from New York, in 1853, to sell canvas tarps and wagon coverings to the rapidly growing population of 49ers who were coming to California looking for gold. Twenty years later, Levi Strauss learned from a Russian-born tailor named Jacob Davis that miners really needed sturdy pants made with rivets at stress points so they would last in rugged conditions. Strauss and Davis jointly patented a new kind of pants, made out of denim, called them blue jeans, and founded an empire. Strauss had the ability, in the Vitality lingo, to explore, changing his business model and evolving to meet the needs of his customers. What would have happened if he had pushed Davis off, telling him that the idea would have never worked? From a psychological standpoint, Strauss had, at a minimum, what organizational scientists call absorptive capacity, which is the ability to learn from your existing environment and transform it into something innovative.

Today, there are lots of other entrepreneurs with capabilities similar to Strauss, creating new and amazing enterprises. These companies, like Google, Uber, and Airbnb, have their own unique challenges, but are growing faster than any companies have historically grown before. Uber is the largest taxi service in the world, yet doesn't own a single taxi. Airbnb is now the largest hospitality company in the world, without owning a single hotel room. Google's highly successful news service is an "accumulator" that collects and displays the news that others have created. Google itself has no news bureau or content providers. The list goes on. The largest retailer in the world today? Alibaba, a Chinese e-commerce company that connects manufacturers, exporters, sellers, and buyers. It carries no inventory, nor does it have any warehouses itself. These companies are enablers, allowing others to provide products and services, rather than organizations that manufacture a product or provide a service of their own. Remember how novel eBay was at the beginning? It was the pioneer in enabling individual sellers to connect directly to buyers. When it grappled with how to build trust into these financial transactions between strangers, PayPal was born.

These companies were all created by people like Strauss, who saw a need for a new kind of business. Thanks in large part to new technologies, they succeeded quickly by exploring new methods of connecting potential customers with suppliers and developing new business models. Traditional hoteliers, taxi services, retailers, and media companies are working hard to try to figure out how to respond. George Zimmer, the founder of Men's Warehouse, announced the formation of zTailors: This website will match you up with local tailors who will come to your house and provide tailoring services at a fixed price. An analysis by Barron's gives the business a decent chance of succeeding and states that there is currently no real competition.

In late nineteenth-century San Francisco, big money was not made by the vast majority of gold miners, but by suppliers to the gold miners, like Strauss. Today, big money seems to be accumulating not for those who make or own goods or property, but for Internet-enabled mediators and connectors like Uber, Airbnb, Alibaba, and eBay. These are the new merchants. Distributed computing and data-collection processes, which rely on the ubiquity of the smartphone, are also growing fast with services like Waze (a start-up bought by Google), which collects data from other Waze users in real time to deliver accurate traffic conditions. Then there's also Pressurenet, a weather application that states on their homepage, "We're connecting smartphone sensors to build the highest-resolution weather data platform available." One can't help but wonder which services or industries will be next.

So what are the common personality traits of these innovative leaders? What similarities are there between Strauss and Davis in the 1800s and people like Airbnb's founder Brian Chesky or Uber co-founders Travis Kalanick and Garret Kamp?

They all successfully explored new domains by developing ideas and systems that were aimed at maximizing the future potential of their firms. But beyond that, they also were able to move those new ideas into territory that maximized Current Performance, allowing them to quickly gain market dominance before competitors could muscle in. They could execute. They developed Future Potential, which they rapidly converted into Current Performance. They demonstrated Vitality. In this chapter, we will explore how to select individuals for specific roles within the Vitality framework, as well as how to develop your own Vitality-oriented abilities.

The Hero Fallacy

Firefighting has a glamorous cachet, with an image of heroes rushing to rescue people from life-threatening situations, as well as the occasional cat or other creature unfortunate enough to get themselves into a hairy predicament. Each time the bell rings and the big trucks pull out, the firefighter's adrenaline begins pumping. And firefighters should be celebrated for their dangerous work, as they provide a very important safety net (sometimes quite literally).

There are some organizations that also celebrate their own heroes, who, like firefighters, rush to the rescue, averting one organizational catastrophe after another, or by taking on the Labors of Hercules to accomplish an important organizational goal. But unlike the celebration that should follow a rescue by a firefighter, an organization's celebratory efforts create a culture that relies on heroes to avert disaster, rather than maximizing Current Performance and putting in place robust processes and procedures to avoid the need for firefighters in the first place.

When in firefighting mode, those in the organization, just like firefighters, feel an adrenaline rush. It may be fun and exhilarating to rush to the rescue. But this will ultimately lead to burn-out and potential disgruntlement about how poorly the organization is being managed. Will there occasionally be the need for firefighting heroes in the organization? Of course. Unusual things happen and their efforts are worthy of celebration. But in the vital organization, the maximization of Current Performance is obtained by having consistent, repeatable processes and procedures of a high quality, which avoid the need for firefighting to occur.

Traits and Individual Characteristics

Employees within a vital organization tend to fall into one of three categories: Executors, Explorers, or Boundary Spanners. Executors are people who maximize Current Performance, allowing the organization to operate efficiently and effectively. They help deliver a company's products and services at high quality for the lowest possible cost by maximizing employee potential, staying focused on goals and targets, and always considering the bottom line. Executors tend to excel at team management by building upon talent, providing mentoring, setting clear and attainable targets, offering feedback, and removing obstacles. Many executors are also customer service-oriented. Executors are invaluable at organizations precisely because of their attention to detail, especially where profit margins are concerned, as well as their ability to enhance team morale and promote organic growth. They serve an organization best when placed in departments with specific targets like sales, operations, and quality controls; roles that involve dealing with internal or external clients like human resources or customer service; or as team managers.

Explorers are people like Strauss, Chesky, Kalanick, and Kamp, who help invent the future for the organization. Explorers focus on which products and services the company will offer, the markets it will exploit, where it will spend its R&D dollars, and how it envisions the future unfolding. They tend to embrace both personal and organizational change, and adapt easily to new situations or environments. Explorers challenge existing paradigms while striving for continual improvement, helping companies realize their Future Potential. They are often self-motivating and creative, and enjoy jobs that allow them to engage in abstract or original thinking. Explorers often recognize serendipitous opportunities and seize them, and thrive in roles that allow them the freedom to explore new directions. These individuals find inspiration in diverse places, thrive in open-learning environments with new technology or capabilities, seize opportunities to innovate or develop new products, and in general do best when they have the autonomy to act on their ideas. Finally, Boundary Spanners are the people who operate with one foot in both of those worlds, following the model of Vitality. Boundary Spanners are critical to enabling Vitality by integrating the work of the Executors and Explorers. In other words, they keep their eye on Current Performance while also looking at the horizon. Boundary Spanners are often highly intelligent and curious by nature. They have a breadth of experiences to rely on when making decisions. Boundary spanners have the ability to deal well with ambiguous situations that don't offer a clear action path. Like Explorers, they are creative, and excel at both thinking of new uses for existing products and services, as well as developing new ones that are completely unique. They can shift from execution to exploration seamlessly. They see how exploration and execution are connected and find opportunities to seek out new possibilities while maintaining present operations. They have a keen sense for how to turn a vague idea into an actionable initiative. Boundary Spanners often have wide networks of friends and colleagues, and demonstrate absorptive capacity, or the ability to absorb and store a large diversity of knowledge that can be drawn on when needed. They are able to connect seemingly disparate pieces of information, experience, and data from various parts of their lives to create novel solutions. They are capable of behavioral complexity, letting them perform the multiple competing roles necessary in Execution and Exploration. Most importantly, they understand the paradox between Current Performance and Future Potential and are willing to tackle it head-on.

Recent research[1] intensively studied those operating in Vitality fashion, utilizing a qualitative methodology. Researchers discovered the following shared personal characteristics[2] among these Vitality-oriented leaders:

- **Openness:** A willingness to seek out new and original ideas, possibilities, or situations.
- **Optimism:** A positive attitude in regards to challenges and the possibility of accomplishment within an organization. These individuals are confident in their abilities and embrace obstacles as learning opportunities.
- **Resiliency:** The ability to learn from failures and easily bounce back from conflict or adversity.
- **Agility:** The ability to adapt to new environments or to shift priorities, goals, or current work based on new information, failures, or obstacles.

[1] Hendrickson, V., "The Traits and Behaviors of Ambidextrous Individuals: How Exploration and Exploitation are Integrated At the Individual Level," (2015).
[2] John, O. P., Donahue, E. M., & Kentle, R. L., "The Big Five Inventory—Versions 4a and 54." (Berkeley, CA: University of California, Berkeley, Institute of Personality and Social Research, 1991).

These individuals are often able to rebalance the relationship between Current Performance and Future Potential whenever necessary.

- **Complex Problem-Solving:** Solving problems systematically, integrating information from multiple sources, and using both short and long term orientations to find solutions.
- **Extraversion**: Acting sociably, energetically, or enthusiastically in any setting. Extraverts often take on leadership roles in group settings.
- **Personal Orientation:** A hyperawareness of oneself and interactions with others because of the meaningful impact these individuals have in any situation. People with personal orientation are often incredibly passionate and persistent.
- **Career Orientation:** Focusing on one's professional development because it relates to self-identity. These individuals set challenging learning and career goals for themselves and then set out to accomplish those goals by taking on additional responsibilities or learning new skills.

Based on the above characteristics, an individual desiring to operate in a vital fashion should seek out new and big challenges, which may often require a new skill set within new contexts. They must make active use of a diversity of personal experiences and opinions, while creating and maintaining clear boundaries between the needs of Current Performance and exploration of Future Potential. They must also integrate and align diverse stakeholders, enabling people with diverse interests to work toward a common goal, as well as refine and focus goals by integrating information from a wide and varied set of inputs. Finally, these individuals gain additional perspectives by collaborating with others both within and outside the organization.

Clearly, this is no easy task. Individuals who are truly emblematic of Vitality—Steve Jobs, Elon Musk, Indra Nooyi—are few and far between. Vital leaders do not necessarily have each of the characteristics described above, although it's an easier path for those who do. Leaders can compensate for any attributes they may be missing, as well as balance their team to incorporate individuals with various qualities on this list. And organizations can offer these leaders specialized support to better empower them. For example, these individuals tend to face many obstacles and failures. Companies can empower these leaders by rewarding their work even when they fail by providing them with mentors or coaches, giving them access to experts, and supporting their long-term goals. Too many companies value employees who merely work at maintaining Current Performance without recognizing the importance of those who focus on Future Potential, because it is harder—and often involves lots of failures—to reap the benefits of that work.

Nature Versus Nurture

Invariably the question will arise: Are people born with the ability to function in a Vitality way or is it something that can be taught? The problem with this question is that it assumes a binary condition: Namely, it is either Nature or Nurture. But as in most things in life, working in a Vitality fashion requires operating along a continuum. While you may be born with certain characteristics and abilities, such as agility or resiliency, you can certainly shape those characteristics and abilities through education, environmental exposure, and the behaviors that you practice. Where you will fall exactly on that continuum of ability can be moved. Most things in life are not binary. You are not simply rich or poor, tall or short, fat or thin, sane or insane. The continuum of normal runs in both directions from the mean. Think, for instance, of organizational skills. Some people may be born with a proclivity towards organization, but for most people, it's a skill that needs to be taught. The average person likely has an average ability to stay organized at work. Over time, your environment and your behaviors can shape your tolerance for sloppy work habits. You can learn to be organized or you can learn to be disorganized. Some of us end up tolerating a good deal of disorganization, at the lower end of the continuum, and others of us are exceedingly fastidious, at the upper end of the continuum. Abnormality is nothing more than distance from the mean, and comes in two flavors: an abundance or a shortage of a characteristic. While you may not have complete control over your characteristics and abilities, you do have the ability to shape them with your efforts.

One characteristic that many successful people have is perseverance. They suffered setbacks and repeated failure on their way to remarkable accomplishment. In one situation, at one point in time, they may have been seen as rather average, or even as failures—George Washington, Abraham Lincoln, Winston Churchill, and Mahatma Gandhi all fall into this category—but when placed in different circumstances, these individuals were able to harness inner resiliency, rise to new challenges, and to succeed beyond all expectation. They were able to shape their behaviors to harness their skills and apply them to new and novel situations.

The Growth Mindset

Are you smart?

Chances are, as a reader of this book, that the answer is yes. But now answer this: Just how much of your success is due to your intelligence or talent?

The way you answer that question greatly affects how you approach a challenge, says Stanford University professor Carol Dweck, author of *Mindset*, which explores why people succeed. According to Dweck's research, those who think that innate intelligence or talent is the driving force behind their success have a fixed mindset, and they see no room for learning or improvement because you either have the ability or not. These people discount the role that effort, luck, or chance play. It is so common in organizations that Dweck nicknamed it the "CEO disease." These people are often afraid to fail because they see it as an indictment of their intelligence or ability, and may veer towards safer, more predictable outcomes as a result.

People are more likely to succeed if they have a growth mindset, believing that their most basic abilities can be developed through dedication and hard work, and that complex problems or obstacles provide us learning opportunities. These are people who are willing to tackle difficult issues because the outcome is not tied to their own self-worth. According to Dweck, people who believe that success comes from effort are also more likely to rebound after failure. They are persistent, willing to try again because they believe that the failure stemmed from either external factors or simply needed more effort, rather than from a fixed trait. Someone who fails and thinks it was a result of just not being smart enough is not motivated to try again.

Clearly, this has big implications for the vital organization, which must rebound quickly from many Future Potential failures. You can cultivate this mindset in your employees by creating a culture that embraces it. To do this, you need to treat failures as learning opportunities by encouraging cooperation and carefully ensuring that employees who pursue various exploration efforts are not subject to any judgment or punishment. This will take some effort, but the payoff—both for individuals and your organization—will be huge.

Organizations: The Sum of Individuals

Organizations are the sum of the individuals laboring within them, and as a result organizations, like people, can change. Given the right tools or staffing, any organization can improve performance. Stripped to the essence, an organization is nothing more than a unifying concept that allows for common purpose and shared activity among its members. Any organization is nothing more than an amalgamation of people, bringing to bear their respective talents and skills for a common and shared purpose. Organizations do not make decisions, provide recognition, or give feedback. They do not hire or fire. Organizations do not decide when and how to maximize Current Performance or when to devote resources to the exploration of new and exciting organizational futures. People do, people who happen to reside within the organizational structure. There are people who try to hide behind organizational structures, but once the structure is stripped away, you are left with people who will determine the actions that the organization will undertake and the methods by which it will operate.

So when we make the assumption that organizations can change, what we are really saying is that people can change. People can be replaced by others with different skill sets, moral codes, operating standards, or other differences. Alternatively, people can change, perhaps by increasing their knowledge or by changing their behaviors. They can change the way they get work done, and they can change the way they interact with others, among other possibilities.

People can change the way an organization functions by changing the policies, practices, and procedures that other members of the organization follow. It is the people inside the organization who must take the initiative to create the change, for the organization itself is incapable of doing that. We are not splitting hairs here, for there is a critical distinction between those who are waiting for an organization to act versus those who realize that it is the people within the organization who must act. Getting the people within the organization to realize that they must take action is half the battle of organizational change.

Translating Individual Characteristics into Organizational Behaviors

Vital organizations don't simply arise spontaneously. They take work and effort, even when the organization is filled with people of incredible talent. The need for practice to achieve consistency in performance is pervasive and critical to operating in Vitality fashion. There will be a strong tendency in organizations towards execution—the maximization of Current Performance—at the expense of building Future Potential or exploring. Only by constant practice, by the relentless pursuit of Vitality, will an organization develop the characteristics necessary for survival and success.

Vitality becomes easier with practice, because it becomes a part of the culture, and less of a struggle for Explorers or Boundary Spanners, who might otherwise find their work unrewarded or even frowned upon. As the organization as a whole becomes more accustomed to Vitality principles, the explorative work of Future Potential becomes more acceptable and welcomed. Individuals also learn to become better Boundary Spanners: They recognize failures and learn from them quickly, they collaborate with stakeholders, and they discover how to convert future-oriented ideas into workable ones that can be executed.

Assessment: Evaluating Your Vitality Team Members

The assessment questions below will help you identify which people in your organization are Executors, Explorers, and Boundary Spanners, and whether your group has the right mix. To take this assessment, first consider the characteristics of those who operate in Vitality fashion: The Boundary Spanners who can maintain a foot in both Current Performance and Future Potential. For each of the statements below, begin by evaluating yourself. Check the items that accurately describe you:

- ○ I am very open to trying new ways of doing things, rather than falling back on the tried and true.
- ○ I tend to be optimistic regarding what my organization can accomplish and what the people within it are capable of.
- ○ If I try something and fail, I tend to rebound quickly.
- ○ I learn from my mistakes, quickly charting an alternative path to accomplish goals.
- ○ I get excited about working on solutions to the toughest problems and biggest challenges my organization faces.
- ○ I get energized by interacting with other people, going out of my way to meet and engage with people I previously did not know.
- ○ I look for the best ideas from people on how to accomplish a challenge, whether they are from within or external to my organization.
- ○ I can sense how others are feeling about a topic and am aware of their needs.
- ○ I am able to persuade people to focus upon and achieve specific goals.
- ○ I set goals for myself, both professional learning goals and career-achievement goals.

How many of these ten statements could you check? You would need a clear majority—six or more—to demonstrate a leaning toward being a Boundary Spanner. While it is important for leaders to have this skill, depending on the work you do, perhaps 5–10% of employees in your organization will need to reflect these characteristics as well. Read through the statements again and try to identify some individuals in your organization who would check even seven or more of the items above. These will be your go-to people to help you balance Current Performance and Future Potential. They will help convert Future Potential explorations into Current Performance execution.

Based on this new understanding of the Boundary Spanners within your organization (or immediate work group), as a second part of this Chap. 4 assessment, check any of the following items that reflect the reality of your organization or your work group specifically:

○ We have in place the dedicated and talented people needed to meet the current demands of our customers or others who depend on our work (i.e., excellent at delivering Current Performance).

○ We have in place the diversity of talent and people who can envision and pursue new ideas in order to develop the products and services we will need in the future (i.e., excellent at building Future Potential).

○ Across all people with varied responsibilities, we have at least 5–10% who could be considered Boundary Spanners (per the 10-item assessment above).

○ Managers consistently understand and monitor the current and the future needs of our customers or those who depend on our work.

○ Managers, or others in a position to do so, notice and sponsor the best ideas for improvements or innovations in order to move them forward.

Were there any of the five statements above that you left unchecked? If so, any unchecked areas reflect areas and needs to address in order to become Vital.

To take this and other assessments online, and get an interactive, customized report, visit OV-CVO.com.

CHAPTER 6

Protecting Innovation

Innovation Rocks!

Humans have been innovating, albeit slowly at first, since at least 3.3 million years ago, when hominids first created crude stone tools. Admittedly, these innovations would be considered simple today, with a rock (called a core) being smashed into another rock to create sharp edges. Some 700,000 years later, humans refined this technique by holding the core in one hand and striking it with a rock held in the other hand, which let the tool maker have more control when making sharp objects. Today, there would be no patience for a 700,000-year innovation project plan, with innovations seemingly coming fast and furious in the sciences, technology, and other areas of discovery. In this chapter, we will cover the importance of innovation to the vital organization, and how to cultivate innovation at your company.

The Innovative Buzz

These days, everyone says they are innovative—or at least they want to be. But what does that mean exactly?

An innovation is anything that is both new *and* useful. Creativity alone is not innovation, but innovation requires using creativity to solve a problem or seize an opportunity. Many think of innovation as merely the creation of new products, but any time a company finds ways to improve performance, processes, or sales, it is an innovation, whether it is a discovery of a better way to sell to customers, or a process change that adds value. You might not be used to thinking about your employees as innovation resources, but if they are indeed your most valuable asset, or if they represent your competitive edge in the marketplace, you should definitely be thinking about how to improve how you hire, retain, deploy, and otherwise organize your staff, and how these approaches can be leveraged both to enable and encourage innovation. Consider innovation as possible across all six domains of the Vitality Model described in Chap. 3: Leadership, Employees, Process, Offerings, Service, and Customers.

Innovation is often described as coming in bursts of brilliant insight. Serendipitous or game-changing breakthroughs do occur, but much more common is the rolling-up-the-sleeves, seemingly endless hard work that leads to incremental innovation. Oftentimes, innovators build on others' groundbreaking work, and many times it's a collaborative effort. Over the long run, this slow build-up to innovation can radically change the way a business operates. Many famous inventions described as deriving from "ah-ha" moments, such as the light bulb, were nothing of the sort. Ask who invented the incandescent light bulb and most people will tell you Thomas Edison. But while Edison played a very important role in the light bulb, there were 22 other inventors working on the bulb before he came along, and others had to continue his work afterwards to make it into the household product still used today. Innovative breakthroughs like the light bulb are often the result of a lot of previous groundwork. Basic innovations often sit dormant until additional development work is done and insights are gained, allowing the innovation to be applied in day-to-day life. But once the groundwork is set, it is not unusual for innovations to occur in multiple organizations, by multiple people, almost simultaneously. Inventions and innovations spread rapidly when the concept, technology, methodology, and acceptance have "ripened" and are now ready to enter the world.

Innovations at Work

Almost every company out there says it wants to be innovative, and many management teams will say they encourage their staff to be innovative because it is the cornerstone of the company's long-term strategy. Yet too often these companies are not actually creating the necessary environment for innovation to occur. Innovation attempts are risky; companies are often reluctant to invest time or money in projects that have a high likelihood of failing, or may simply not recognize the ideas that are worth pursuing. But without the ability to fail, learn, and try again, employees can shy away from true innovation and avoid anything remotely risky. Unfortunately, if all you do are sure-bet projects, you are not going to achieve true innovation. To learn how to measure whether you, or your company, are truly being innovative, see Chap. 7, "Evaluating Vitality."

An organization's tolerance for risk is a construct that exists in its culture, and in the minds, habits, and activities of employees. Employee surveys are well suited to evaluate how well the stage is set for innovation. Critical components of this "innovation climate" will include:

- Generating innovative ideas;
- The ability to test out those ideas from a funding and other resource standpoint;
- The ability to evaluate innovations to see which ones should be implemented organization-wide and which ones quickly rejected (the concept of fail fast);
- The ability to insert an innovation into the work or product stream and then to quickly standardize it, so that the innovation becomes consistently applied or produced.

How can you know if you are setting yourself up to be as innovative as possible? How do you judge progress on your innovation priorities? The next chapter provides a full treatment on evaluating Vitality, along with the innovations that improve Current Performance or Future Potential. For the moment, however, know that measuring innovation is not as simple as counting patents or sizing up an R&D budget. The focus of this chapter is on the precursors of innovation—the conditions that support the creative application of new solutions to challenges.

To be fair to companies, it's difficult to allow for true innovation. It requires focused funding, flexibility, and the willingness to risk and to fail. But ultimately, the issue is that most leaders *think* they are encouraging innovation, but are stopping short of creating the conditions for innovation or rewarding employees for innovative behaviors regardless of outcome.

Requirements for Innovation

Slack and redundancy are critical for an organization to innovate successfully. If an organization is being run in a very tight fashion, with no slack or extra resources, it can't try new things, and the ability to innovate will not exist.

Likewise, if the organization does not have the ability to experiment with new methods while another redundant process is performing in a traditional fashion, the generation of innovative ideas and processes will be very difficult indeed.

Years ago, a roller-bearing manufacturer was assessing whether a component of the bearing could be produced by forcing powdered metal into a mold under high pressure, or if the traditional method of stamping them out of sheet metal was still best. The new powdered metal-manufacturing line was laid out, and the resulting components were extensively tested against traditionally manufactured components to determine which were best. Slack was available (having the extra resources to try the new method), as well as redundancy (having the two methods both running simultaneously for side-by-side comparisons). Because the company could not risk its entire production capacity on this new approach, it required slack and redundancy to "protect" its innovation effort.

Slack and redundancy are only possible if an organization has more money—from Current Performance products or services—than the day-to-day requirements of running the business require. As we discussed in Chap. 4, it's the integration of Current Performance and Future Potential that allows for innovation. Companies can generate financial resources for innovation by maximizing Current Performance; This means producing products or delivering services cost-effectively and at a quality level that meets or exceeds the standards that customers require or that adhere to regulations. This will generate money above and beyond what is needed to keep the doors open, allowing for the exploration and the building of Future Potential opportunities. Some examples of industries where companies maximized their Current Performance in order to generate the profits required for Future Potential include call centers that moved their operations to India or Ireland, back office support centers in Poland, and manufacturing companies that use factories in China. Many organizations fail to innovate because they simply cannot generate the cash necessary to accomplish this.

Protecting Innovation

Since innovation requires resources and risks, it's necessary to implement procedures to protect it within organizations. Daily issues often take precedence over future orientation because the natural tendency in today's fast-paced environment is to focus on immediate needs. (Of course, this problem is not limited to organizational life. How many people do you know who keep their New Year's Resolutions or save sufficiently for retirement?) Yet if tomorrow's environment is different than the one you are currently operating within, you will be ill-prepared to deal with it. To paraphrase French author François de la Rochefoucauld, the only thing constant in "organizational" life is change. This is a challenge that every organization faces.[1] This chapter highlights things that an organization can do to protect innovation.

The challenge of innovation is compounded by a tumultuous environment. Rapid change in the global marketplace, in technological development, and with shortened product life-cycles all make adaptation more important, yet make learning more difficult. The most effective organizations develop the competencies to respond to this challenge of evolving, while not overly disrupting operations that are well suited to the current environment.

What Kinds of Innovation Most Need Protection?

Figuring out how to protect and nurture innovation first requires breaking down the concept into chunks. As previously mentioned, innovation can refer to any of the six domains in the Vitality model. Within these domains, there are two major kinds of innovation. For the sake of simplicity, let's call the first "Small i" innovation. This refers to incremental innovations that improve Current Performance by streamlining processes, refining products, or adapting services offered. The second, or "Big I" innovation, is about building Future Potential by creating radical or transformative changes, or by creating entirely new capabilities. "Big I" innovation is a more radical transformation of how you operate and what you produce.

For instance, a daycare that more closely matches its operating hours with customer needs is creating"Small i" innovation. But a daycare that expands its services to include senior daycare, opening up new markets to explore and expand into, is doing "Big I" innovation. "Small i" innovation involves slight changes or streamlining "within the box" or current paradigm. "Big I" innovation involves breakthrough changes. It requires thinking—and implementing—"outside the box" or current paradigm. See Fig. 6.1, which breaks down these different kinds of innovation.

[1] March, J. "Exploration and Exploitation in Organizational Learning," *Organizational Science*, 1991.

Improving Current Performance (*Little "i"* **Innovation**)		Building Future Potential (*Big "I"* **Innovation**)
Incremental change	↔	Breakthrough change
Focused on existing products, services	↔	Creates new products, services
Addresses defined problems	↔	Follows creative, playful exploration
Within paradigm	↔	Paradigm-busting
Requires attention, time, resources	↔	Requires significant time, attention, resources
Difficult to maintain efforts	↔	Very difficult to maintain efforts

Fig. 6.1   Two kinds of innovation

"Small i" innovation should happen everywhere within your organization. All processes, products, services, policies, and workflows can always be improved. You are likely familiar with some of the specific disciplines aimed at streamlining Current Performance, which started with Frederick Taylor's time-and-motion study approach published in his *Principles of Scientific Management* in 1911, and is the province of significantly evolved and refined approaches like Total Quality Management, Lean Business Process Engineering, Six Sigma, and a host of other formal disciplines focused on improving efficiencies. More importantly, "Small i" innovation is conceived and implemented by observant and thoughtful employees everywhere, with or without any coaching or authority. This is important, and should be nurtured.

However, the real difficulty is maintaining transformational "Big I" innovation efforts. These innovations, which build Future Potential, require investment, experimentation, risk, and failure on the path to success. This can disrupt Current Performance by introducing a certain amount of chaotic change or diversion of resources away from operations. Organizational leaders need to attend to how they make these investments. Do you simply set loose your most creative and inventive people on a problem? Do you give them a focus and structure, or just let them operate without constraints?

The answer is that you need at least some structure: Goals, objectives, or tools to help explore new possibilities. Creativity works better with at least some constraints. Consider jazz great Duke Ellington, who said, "Without a deadline, baby, I wouldn't do nothing!" If such a renowned jazz musician acknowledges the need for a schedule and goals, we need to listen.

So where should the focus be within your organization? The short answer rests with the questions posed in Chap. 4: What business are you in? Building

Future Potential must align with what your purpose is, and often helps you evolve that purpose as you work toward achieving Vitality, even if you stretch and re-define that purpose.

Who should be most involved in "Big I" innovation to build Future Potential? From where in your organization will the *next big thing* emerge? Will it be from an R&D group, such as is common in pharmaceutical research? Will it be from a fiercely visionary leader like Steve Jobs? Will it bubble up through an internal grass-roots movement like Post-It Notes at 3M? Or will it more organically spawn from "those guys who walk around with their eyes bugging out"?[2] The rest of this chapter reviews various sources of breakthrough innovation, and how organizations can increase the odds of making it happen.

Organizational Structure

Organizations often adapt their structures to protect innovation, specifically the kind of innovation that is focused on new products or services. These companies often have specific innovation-focused groups, known by names such as R&D, New Ventures, Product Development, or Emerging Markets. These are groups with the assignment, and appropriate funding, to find ways to create the products, services, and markets of tomorrow. This is known as "structural separation," a differentiated structure where certain units like operations or sales deliver on Current Performance by working in an efficient and cost-effective manner, possibly with little slack or redundancy, while other units concentrate on the innovations necessary to move the organization into the future. Also, within a given function, there may be some separation of sub-functions. Support functions within organizations may utilize this kind of structural separation. For example, both accounting and finance operate under the CFO, but whereas accounting uses established rules focused on efficiency, finance is aimed at creatively investing in the future. Inside human resources, departments are often split between HR Operations, which deals with the fundamentals of people-related information and processes, and Organizational Effectiveness groups, which cultivate advisory relationships with internal customers to improve leadership, culture, or the connections of HR and "people" strategies with overall business strategies. This kind of

---

[2] This was the description given by one Fortune 100 executive when asked where innovation comes from.

structural separation works well, but only if there are also efforts to integrate the two pieces. One approach to integration is to have employees in key positions who are Boundary Spanners, as described in Chap. 5, who will naturally work to keep the Future Potential efforts aligned with what can eventually fold into Current Performance processes. The most critical requirement for integration, however, is the leadership coordination at the top of these separated structures. Wherever Current Performance (e.g., operations) and Future Potential (e.g., R&D) structures come together on the organizational chart, that point of leadership needs to be exceptionally focused on Vitality and keeping the two efforts aligned.

The research highlights advantages to structural separation, but, as alluded to above, only if done correctly. In a seminal *Harvard Business Review* article in 2004,[3] Stanford professor Charles O'Reilly and Harvard professor Michael Tushman reviewed 35 attempts to launch breakthrough innovations across nine different industries. Their goal was to determine which of the following four basic organizational structures best supported this development of Future Potential. The structures they evaluated were:

1. Functional Design: This is a traditional approach, where each separate entity or department is specialized, and reports up through top management-level leaders. The project teams for the emerging innovations in this study were also a part of this existing structure, operating within their own group or department and reporting up to management, without any specific accommodations made for the innovation effort.

2. Cross-Functional Teams: These are teams that represent a blend of individuals from various functions across the organizations studied. Members come from existing departments like manufacturing, sales, and R&D, but they did not report to the heads of those departments, and may not have a clear, authoritative channel into the top management of the organization.

3. Unsupported Teams: This is an approach that fully separates the individuals involved in creating the various innovations being examined. These are groups set up fully outside the established organizational and management hierarchy, with no collaboration or shared resources.

[3] O'Reilly & Tushman, "The Ambidextrous Organization," *Harvard Business Review,* 2004.

4. Ambidextrous Organizations: These organizations are separate from the day-to-day functioning of the organization, yet still integrated into the overall strategy through direct reporting relationships to top leadership. In this structure, emerging businesses have their own functional structure, such as independent manufacturing, sales, or R&D. However, they report to an executive who is tightly integrated with the leadership team of the existing businesses.

O'Reilly and Tushman wanted to know the success rate of each of the four structures. The results were clear: More than 90% of the innovation efforts within the Ambidextrous Organizational structures met their goals, whereas only about a quarter of the functional designs produced real innovation, and none of the cross-functional or unsupported teams succeeded. As an example, O'Reilly and Tushman describe the emergence of USAToday.com, which initially launched in 1995 as a completely separate entity from the print publication. Despite the booming Internet economy, the new venture floundered in part because it was regarded as competition by *USA Today's* print staff. Additionally, as this was originally an independent organization, it did not have access to the larger organization's resources. Tom Curley, then the president and publisher of *USA Today*, realized that the emerging online business needed to nestle alongside the existing print business, and even the television network stations that were also part of the larger organization. He completely restructured the organization, replacing senior leaders who opposed a more integrated organization, and instituted daily editorial meetings that cut across the different divisions. News reporting could be leveraged across television, online, and print channels, yet still maintain the young and fast-paced culture of new media. According to Curley, "We're no longer in the newspaper business; we're in the news information space, and we'd better learn to deliver content regardless of form." In other words, he redefined their business to incorporate breakthrough innovation.

The advantages of this Ambidextrous Organizational structure enable management to align and integrate with the overarching priorities of the organization, to cross-pollinate ideas, to leverage organizational resources, and to maintain constructive relationships across organizational boundaries. Yet the separation enables the emergent business to develop its own styles and structure, and be free from the day-to-day production realities of the existing business. Similarly, the existing business can be shielded from the tumult of a new business launch.

It's important to note that O'Reilly and Tushman's research focused on large-scale launches of new businesses, where the original creative spark had already been established, like USAToday.com, and the primary work was to implement that idea successfully. Smaller-scale efforts, or those earlier in their evolution, will need to find correspondingly "smaller" versions of the Ambidextrous Organization structure. Consider the ball-bearing manufacturer mentioned above. They achieved the same tone as the Ambidextrous Organization structure without a total organizational redesign, but with a more focused separation across manufacturing lines within a single plant.

What about fully structurally separate, free-form think tanks? Google Labs, for example, was originally created to enable new and creative ideas—both large and small—to find a place in their products and services. It sounded like a great idea, and in fact produced features incorporated into Gmail and other services used by millions. However, as a part of an increased organizational focus ("More wood behind fewer arrows," according to CEO Larry Page), Google officially closed the Labs in July of 2011. In a post on Google's official blog that month, SVP for Research and Systems Infrastructure Bill Coughran wrote, "While we've learned a huge amount by launching very early prototypes in Labs, we believe that greater focus is crucial if we're to make the most of the extraordinary opportunities ahead." In the end, Google Labs was like the Unstructured Team structure described above—not sufficiently integrated into the overall organization's strategy and focus.

Whatever the organizational structure and the attempts to provide buffers from day-to-day concerns, the broader lessons are these:

1. Create a buffer from day-to-day realities so that those involved with developing and implementing Future Potential can focus without distraction;
2. Maintain the right executive-level sponsorship and involvement to stay connected to organizational strategy and priorities; and
3. Enable the right kinds of boundary-spanning to cross-pollinate, share resources, and stay calibrated with the most important stakeholders.

Mergers and Acquisitions

Rather than build new capabilities internally, some organizations choose to buy them. An acquired company is, up until the moment of integration, a completely separate structure. For big corporations, the legions of smaller start-up companies can represent an opportunity to manage the risk of failure inherent in innovation. Among technology start-ups in particular, roughly 90% fail because the product or service they produce could not find customers. Many established companies may not want to do all the required work for a 10% success rate, so instead sit back and wait for smaller companies to succeed or fail, and then swoop in and acquire innovation through selective acquisitions.

Acquisitions are also used to expand Current Performance by enlarging territories, customer lists, production, or service capacity. When the objective of the acquisition is tied to an organization's Future Potential strategy, however, the purchases are much more difficult, the stakes are higher, and the chance of success decreases. But you can apply the lessons from the previous organizational-structure discussion to help integrate strategic acquisitions. Assume for the moment that *USA Today* purchased an online news outlet instead of building their own. What should they have done? In fact, because they originally built USAToday.com as an independent, unsupported team, it was almost like an external organization. But to realize the parent organization's need to move from newspapers to news information, an Ambidextrous Organizational structure was required. The two entities had separate functions, yet needed integration at the executive-leadership level. This is the right answer regardless of whether the business was home-grown or acquired.

Clearly, acquisitions come in all shapes and sizes, and strategic goals vary. But the core advice is not to confuse acquisitions made to improve Current Performance with acquisitions designed to build Future Potential. Current Performance-related acquisitions can be more traditionally integrated. Future Potential-related acquisitions benefit from following the Ambidextrous Organization structure. But however you integrate, it's imperative to maintain the right executive-level sponsorship and involvement to keep the new business connected to organizational priorities, and to enable the right kinds of boundary-spanning to cross-pollinate, share resources, and calibrate the two organizations.

Programs to Nurture Innovation

Internal-structure overhauls or external acquisitions can certainly influence innovation, as mentioned in the previous sections. However, those major organizational efforts are only part of the innovation toolkit. We describe other programs implemented by various companies to help nurture creativity and innovation below:

Split Time-Innovation Program Popularized by Google's "20% Time," these programs are based on the concept that employees complete their traditional job, yet save a portion of time (typically 10–20%) for innovation. This time is not monitored or measured, but free, unconstrained time to be creative, and to experiment and play. These programs sound good, but their maintenance depends on a supportive organizational culture. Clearly they are expensive, reducing the traditional output of employees by up to one day's worth of work in a typical five-day workweek. Over the long term, these programs bring benefit to the organization via viable innovations, and professional development to the employees who participate. For them to be successful, participation should be limited to employees who are able to balance multiple complex tasks and demonstrate the characteristics of Vitality (see Chap. 5). Participants should have access to support, and have some guidelines—such as check-in groups or regular reports—to help structure their ambiguous goals.

Blitz Day A health-care organization tasked certain employees, dubbed ambassadors, with reaching out in person to every single employee in the organization on one specific day. These ambassadors went to every facility the organization owned or operated, greeting employees and giving them a piece of candy, along with a card instructing them to think of one idea to improve patient care or customer service, and then share it with their manager. The ambassador then moved on to the next employee, keeping focused on the task. According to the organization, every employee, from the top doctor down to lab technicians and receptionists, was greeted and given a card. Connecting with every single employee—thus proving the company's commitment to really listening to their ideas—sent a powerful message, helped create buzz, and ultimately propelled this health-care organization from being ranked last in employee satisfaction to first during a ten-year period. This is how a cultural shift starts. Indeed, employees discussed the Blitz Day for years afterwards, and it has become part of company lore.

Ideas from Everywhere Competition CareerBuilder launches a competition every couple of years, inviting employees to submit ideas and a business plan for new products. This is not a quick effort. Typically a six-month process, employees participating in the competition meet throughout this time with an assigned leader for guidance in molding an initial idea into a business plan. There are templates and resources for how to construct the plan. Up to 50 submissions are reviewed, and the top 10 finalists present their proposal to top leadership. Besides the honor, the winning participant may get resources to develop the idea into a full-fledged project. Not all winning ideas convert into products, but there are products that exist today because of this contest. The winners have come from a variety of backgrounds within the company, including technology, human resources, senior managers, new employees, and front-line employees.

Hack-a-Thons Born out of the high-tech programming community, a Hack-a-Thon is typically a 24-hour period where employees are freed from traditional job duties and encouraged to work as individuals or in teams on whatever pet project they want. The organization might provide food and games around the clock to maintain a festive and playful atmosphere. The event concludes with an informal show-and-tell where people report about what they worked on and what they learned. Top ideas might be officially given time from leadership to be explored further. But most of the time, the benefit is intrinsic to employees as a time to play and explore new possibilities. The goal is creative freedom. Hack-a-Thons are easier to implement when many people are in a single location, though worldwide or virtual participation is encouraged. A variation on Hack-a-Thons takes prospective employees, those who want jobs at the organization, and gives them an opportunity to show the organization what they've got. The top-performing Hack-a-Thon participants are then offered positions with the company.[4]

These types of programs are just a sampling of the special efforts organizations make to nurture innovation. They are more specialized than more traditional off-site brainstorming sessions or training programs. More than the program itself, the big lessons they share are the following:

1. They create special allocations of time to work on or share ideas. Like an annual New Year's resolution, these programs create opportunities for employees to step out of the day-to-day and focus on and discuss new ideas.
2. They create "buzz" and stories within the organization. Whether a Blitz Day or a Hack-a-Thon event, these are activities that get talked about and endure as symbols of the organization's culture.
3. They represent organizational priorities, sharing company values with employees. With the Blitz Day, a topic is provided, such as patient care or customer satisfaction. With the other programs, it is the opportunity to be creative that is the big message. Some built-in access to leadership reinforces these priorities.
4. They create a common language and culture of innovation.
5. With repetition, they create a rhythm to look forward to. Like exercise or advertising, a single occurrence has little effect. Integration into an organization's annual calendar is where the impact really lies.

[4] "What The Hack?" *The Economist*, Dec 5, 2015.

To protect innovation, doing any specific program listed here is not what is important. But doing *something* is critical. What you choose depends on your organization.

Assessment: Evaluating Your Innovation Efforts

Since time and resources devoted to Future Potential are all too often distracted by day-to-day concerns, this assessment focuses on the special efforts that you make (whether changes in structures, practices, policies, motivation, etc.) in order to protect innovation. With the statements below, check off all items that apply to your organization:

○ We successfully live up to our own innovation aspirations regarding how we streamline Current Performance ("Small i" innovation).

○ We successfully live up to our own innovation aspirations regarding how we build Future Potential ("Big I" innovation).

○ We have the capacity (people, time, and resources) to act on promising new or innovative ideas.

○ Sufficient attention gets devoted to innovation efforts, and is buffered from the press of day-to-day concerns.

○ Our organizational structure (including job assignments and formal accountabilities) helps to "protect" innovation efforts sufficiently, yet keeps them aligned with business realities.

○ We effectively buy/acquire and integrate innovation (either to streamline Current Performance or build Future Potential), whether small-scale or more significant acquisition.

○ We have successful programs and explicit efforts to protect and nurture innovation (i.e., formal rhythms to set aside time regularly for employees to be creative, free from operational concerns, as opposed to a less effective "go innovate" directive).

Organizations as a whole, or work groups responsible for breakthrough innovation, need to clearly see all seven of these statements in operation. If you endorsed five or six items, then your priorities for improvement are clear. If you checked fewer than five items, your ability to build Future Potential may be compromised. This can be a temporary situation, but would eventually need to be addressed to avoid stagnation.

To take this and other assessments online, and get an interactive, customized report, visit OV-CVO.com.

CHAPTER 7

Evaluating Vitality

Ants Go Marching

Raiding swarms of army ants move in a coordinated fashion, following trails of pheromones laid down by the preceding ants, searching for food. Most ants simply follow the other ants, eventually obtaining food and bringing it back for the colony. But about 1% are pioneer ants, who stray from the path and chart new territory. Most pioneer ants die, but the ones that survive find new sources of food, and the trails that they create will ultimately become the paths for the rest of the colony. In this way, pioneer ants ensure the survival of the colony by always leading the ants to new sources of food.

Just like an organization, these colonies survive because of the interdependence of these two types of ants: The worker ants and the pioneer ants. And just as scientists measure various aspects of the ants' work habits, so too can we measure both Current Performance and Future Potential. However, the metrics used will be different. Consider the ants: You cannot compare how efficiently the worker ants gather food with how well the pioneer ants find it in the first place, but that doesn't make the work of the pioneer ants any less necessary. The key is discovering the best ways to measure Current Performance and Future Potential, and using those measurements to understand the cycle of exploration and execution as Future Potential becomes Current Performance.

The Organization as Omnivore

An omnivore has certain advantages. Since it's not a picky eater, an omnivore can wander away from its traditional food source and expect that it will find something to eat when it gets to wherever it is going. However, when an omnivore crosses into new or unexplored territory and comes across completely foreign food it faces a dilemma. The omnivore's dilemma—as explained by Paul Rozin[1]—essentially states that omnivores must find new foods and new food sources as they move around, but at the same time use caution until the safety of the food source is proven. Is this new food something that it can safely eat, or is it a food, like certain wild mushrooms, that should be avoided at all costs? How can it know and how does it decide whether to risk it?

New York University Professor Jonathan Haidt[2] describes omnivores as having two competing drives or motives: neophilia, an attraction to new things, and neophobia, a fear of new things. In humans, neophilia and neophobia are not binary conditions, but rather exist along a spectrum, with each term anchoring one end of the "neo" scale. People who score higher on neophilia are more open to new experiences, including meeting new people and considering new ideas. Neophobic people do not like new experiences, preferring tradition, and guarding borders and boundaries that can be either physical or social.

According to Haidt, an omnivore's ability to survive as it wanders into new territory or attempts to utilize new food sources depends upon its having evolved a disgust emotion or reaction to elements in the environment that could prove deadly, such as a dangerous food source. Omnivore flexibility only goes so far. For instance, you would be hard pressed to find an omnivore that would eat rotting meat, as only very specialized types of animals, like vultures, can manage that without getting sick. Disgust, as it turns out, is also not binary, but exists along a continuum, along with neophobia and neophilia. Neophobics tend to have a more readily triggered disgust mechanism.

Organizations face the omnivore's dilemma continually. Do they "try new foods" by hiring leaders from the outside, exposing themselves to potentially new ideas and new ways of doing business, which might lead the company to new successes but could potentially prove poisonous instead? Or do they promote from within, utilizing those who have risen from the ranks, have found

[1] Rozin, P., & Haidt, J. "The Domains of Disgust and their Origins: Contrasting Biological and Cultural Evolutionary Accounts," *Trends in Cognitive Science*, 17, 367–368, 2013.
[2] Haidt, J., *The Righteous Mind: Why Good People are Divided by Politics and Religion*, (Knopf Doubleday, 2012).

success with the organization's current methods and processes, and are deeply imbued with the organization's existing culture and ways of doing things? That is a surefire method of guarding one's social and physical boundaries, which might lead to the continuation of a success story, but could alternatively cause a stagnant organization to become obsolete in the face of environmental or market changes. If the leader of the organization is neophobic or neophiliac, will it affect which path he or she chooses?

If one organization acquires another organization, do they take the best of both cultures, processes, and procedures in order to forge a brand new entity, or do they bend the newly acquired organization to the will, culture, and methods or processes of the acquirer? Do they guard their borders or are they open to new experiences and the ideas of new people?

As organizations consider which products to bring to market, which markets to enter, or how to grow in their existing markets, they have choices regarding when to stick to the tried-and-true and when to strike out in search of the new. One path is not inherently safer or more guaranteed than the other, for both paths carry risks. How you choose which path to take depends on your need at the moment. Current Performance issues often can be solved "closer to home," with existing structures or tools. Future Performance-related problems may require more exploration and out-of-the-box thinking. Organizations cannot operate too far to one side of the neophobia versus neophilia spectrum, but rather must have a healthy mix of the two in order to best face challenges.

Organizational Needs for Measuring Current Performance

Why do organizations measure performance? Simple: It offers a chance for change and improvement. This is true whether the organization measures an individual's performance (with performance evaluations), a group's effectiveness (such as same-store sales growth), or overall organizational success (like market share). Performance evaluations should prompt individuals to perform better and enable decisions that promote the best. Monthly sales reports should reinforce successful practices and guide investments in weaker areas. An understanding of market-share trends can help evaluate product lifecycles, and where to invest in renewal or divest aged or irrelevant efforts.

However, knowing what to measure—and how best to measure it—is complex. Too often, people rely only on metrics, which are a set of measurements that quantify specific results. Yet for business purposes, it is important to factor in other kinds of evidence-based information. Instead of creating lists of possible things to measure, start with the fundamental goal of improvement. First, consider the three questions of Vitality—two of which should be familiar by now—to figure out what measurements are necessary for the improvements you are striving to make:

1. What is our Current Performance—our ability to earn money and conduct the basic operations of the organization—and how will it play into our future?
2. How are we building Future Potential—new kinds of value driven by a unique strategy—that will keep us relevant, and what do we think this will look like in the future?
3. How good are we at turning Future Potential explorations into well-executed Current Performance, and how quickly do we accomplish this?

Answering these questions can be tricky, but is necessary in the quest to make better, evidence-based decisions—such as who to promote, where to invest, how to adapt strategy, and so on. In order to answer them, companies should draw from several sources of evidence:

1. **Empirical- or metrics-based research from other organizations:** Empirical evidence comes from observation or experience. In this case, the information is gathered from scientific or management literature or research done within other organizations, rather than at your company, and provides a good starting point.
2. **Best practices from other organizations:** These are professional procedures from other companies that are widely accepted as being the most effective or efficient, and are often used as a benchmark for measurement.
3. **Specific metrics and indicators:** These are quantifiable measurements, created within your organization, to assess certain aspects of your business.
4. **Professional expertise and judgment:** This is reliance on the extensive knowledge of certain individuals within your organization who may have background or expertise in a specific area, as well as trained

decision-makers, who can properly interpret research, best practices, and metrics.

5. **Perspectives of stakeholders:** Stakeholders are any individuals or companies with an interest in your organization. These individuals or groups can contribute an alternative perspective to any decisions with significant impact on others, such as hiring employees, choosing suppliers, or winning customers.

6. **Intuition or leap of faith:** Ultimately, all the above forms of evidence simply guide your decision-making ability. You will always need to go beyond evidence to conclude whether or not a decision will be the right one, because metrics and other evidence will never create a locked-down recipe for success, especially in the future, when the dynamics of a successful decision can be very different from those in the past. The goal is to structure your intuitive decision or leap of faith within the available evidence in order to reach the best possible conclusion.

Evaluating Current Performance

All these information sources should be used to evaluate your company's Current Performance. Choosing which sources of information to use, and how heavily to rely on them, depends upon the specific aspects of your business that you intend to measure. When choosing what is right for the task at hand, keep in mind that the Current Performance objective is to streamline your operations from beginning to end.

Consider manufacturing: Any company involved in manufacturing should always strive to produce more units in less time, with less waste of resources, fewer defects, and with less downtime in the production line. These are all types of efficiency metrics, which reduce costs to the organization. They usually imply increasing control, standardization, and routinization. There will be historical trends to evaluate. There may be multiple manufacturing sites to compare. There will be patterns in customer orders that can be predicted, with more intimate involvement with the largest customers. There may even be competitive information from similar organizations that can provide general guidelines about scrap rates, workplace injuries, or costs of delivery.

There are some fundamental principles to make sure your measurements and other evidence to evaluate Current Performance stay constructive and on track. First, look beyond readily available or obvious metrics. Often, the measurement of performance starts with what is available, rather than what makes sense. It is easy to be seduced by a clean, available, and well-understood number that does not actually reflect what you are trying to accomplish. Take an easy example from the discipline of employee opinion surveys: Too often, surveys are judged based on the response rate, rather than the improvements they prompt. Response rates are instead an indicator of a survey's execution, not the topics they are covering, and they certainly do not reflect *why* the survey exists in the first place. An imperfect, not-quite-quantifiable indicator of any advancement made as a result of the survey would be much better than a clear and quantifiable metric that does not factor into a company's quest for improvement.

Second and related, separate the process of measurement from the eventual outcome. Too often, individuals may become infatuated with predictors and lose sight of the original target. Take a hospital looking to measure how long it takes for a patient to actually leave the hospital after a doctor orders a discharge. The hospital may measure the time between when the order is submitted in the computer and when the patient actually vacates the room. This will be a clear, easily understood number. But what does it mean? Pretend the hospital learns that the average wait time is four hours. Leaders from this organization may say they need to cut this wait time for faster turnover. But they haven't learned the reason for the delay. Maybe it takes too long to enter the discharge information, to get medicine from the pharmacy, or simply to deliver the discharge papers to the patient. Either way, the outcome—trying to cut the time between discharge and actual leaving—gets muddled.

When you become infatuated with the process or even the specific measurement, it is too easy to lose sight of what you are trying to do. To prevent this, start with your unique problem or challenge, taking care not to jump too quickly to a potential solution. Then evaluate the tools you use to measure performance. People may mistakenly focus on the wrong problem because of the tool at their disposal. (Imagine you have a hammer. Chances are you will look around for the nail. However, your problem may actually be a screw.) You can avoid this by breaking down metrics into those that evaluate efficiency (using resources well), effectiveness (meeting the intended objectives), and impact (the extent that actions have the intended consequences).

Traditionally, impact is the most important, yet hardest to measure, and as a result many people gravitate toward the easier, more understandable metrics of efficiency and effectiveness. Going back to the hospital example from above: It is easier for the organization to measure the efficiency or speed of discharge, but it is both harder and more important to measure the *effectiveness* of discharge, namely that patients are leaving with needed medicines or a follow-up plan for treatment.

People are prone to focus on what they know best, and this can lead to misguided measurements. Again, consider the hammer: If that's the tool you are most familiar with, chances are it's the tool you will gravitate toward. Individuals are likely to frame evaluations within the confines of their discipline. (Not even scientists are immune to this; many are guilty of being "predictor-focused" rather than "criterion-focused.") A classic example of this problem is illustrated by the popularity of employee engagement in the workplace. While there is no question that employee engagement is a worthwhile pursuit—few would want to work in a place where people were not engaged in their work—it has come to be viewed as a singular point of focus through which all good things flow. Do you want more satisfied hotel guests? So-called experts will tell you to engage your employees. Less shrinkage in your retail store? Engage your employees. Better coordination among your symphony musicians or professional basketball players? Engage your employees. This knee-jerk solution to any problem neglects so many other factors contributing to the desired outcome. Lastly, actively evaluate whether the metric produces the behavior change you want.

A United Kingdom hospital learned a difficult lesson when it strove to improve emergency room wait times by measuring the time between patient registration and visits with a doctor. While this sounds reasonable, and in fact did change the behavior of the hospital staff, it did so in a very twisted way. Facing pressure to improve their metrics, the staff delayed patient registration for incoming ambulances until a doctor was available—basically gaming the system rather than creating genuine improvements in patient care. As a result, the metrics showed improvement. However the patient care did not change, except possibly for the worse, as those in urgent need may have faced increased delays. The possibility of mischief and a dark side to metrics is real, and companies need to tread carefully when choosing metrics to avoid situations like this. Here, the hospital tracked the implementation, realized the problem, and was able to adjust by de-emphasizing the single metric (speed of intake), and focusing instead on the ultimate impact (better patient care)

Better Predictions about Current Performance Outcomes

Identifying what kinds of metrics logically reflect Current Performance is important. But how does that connect—beyond theory—to *actual* performance? *Actual* impact? Here, we turn to four research-based analytical methods developed to predict Current Performance so that companies are able to get a better sense of how their Current Performance products or services will hold up in the future:

1. **Machine learning:** Ability of a computer to improve its own performance, enabling it to make predictions on future outcomes based on real data from the past
2. **Big data:** Information that is so vast it cannot be analyzed using standard tools of measurement, tied to the belief that the volume and variety of data will enable previously invisible trends and insights to emerge.
3. **Predictive analytics:** Taking information from existing data sources and predicting patterns or future outcomes.
4. **Linkage research:** The statistical demonstration of relationships between different facets of the business, such as between employee opinions and customer satisfaction.

Each of these pursuits represents a different approach and methodology, yet they all share a common objective: To identify drivers of future success. They each start with the examination of cases or examples of success. These cases can be individually effective decisions, profitable retail stores, high-performing individuals, or satisfying and efficient call-center interactions.

However, looking only at success is insufficient. If we stop there, we fall prey to one of the most prevalent biases in business thinking today: survivorship bias. Any business books, seminars, case studies, best practices, or focus groups that only review success stories or winners will be heavily prone to erroneous conclusions based on this bias.

Consider this: Suppose you want to learn how lottery winners get their tickets. There is an intuitive logic and elegance to learning how to do this by focusing on the winners. If you did focus exclusively on the winners, what would you learn? Perhaps the best advice is to buy your ticket on a Tuesday, choose lotto numbers relevant to a loved one's birthday, or wear special, lucky socks. Or better yet, you might follow the advice of one of the winners of Spain's Christmas lottery, one of the biggest in the world. This recent winner chose a lottery number ending in 48, because he dreamt of the number seven for seven straight nights. And as he said, "Seven times seven is 48."

If you only interviewed the winners, you might take to wearing lucky clothes or performing basic arithmetic incorrectly. The same risk of this "survivorship bias" is seen in interviews of Olympic gold medalists. Often you might conclude that athletic success has to do with coaching, teamwork, perhaps equipment, and so on. You would not hear them talk about other elements that are necessary for their success: Genetics, body type, or the other gifts with which they were born. Whether with lottery winners or Olympic athletes, your conclusions may discount luck, external environmental effects, genetics, or other long-established factors.

To avoid this survivorship bias, an honest evaluation of success in business needs to compare success with failure, or higher performance with lower performance. Machine learning takes this a step beyond intuitive analysis to statistically compare possible indicators of performance and identify those that most differentiate between high and low performance.

Linkage research, in connecting different kinds of data sets (like service climate from an employee survey and customer loyalty from a client survey), can articulate strategic choices, inform decision making, and highlight challenges or areas of risk. Sample findings from work in this area highlight research-based lessons for how metrics interplay with one another. This process pinpoints how organizations can improve. Here are some examples of organizations using these various methods:

- The US National Weather Service identified that weather stations that did a better job encouraging employee creativity and empowerment in decision-making gave significantly more lead time in calling tornado warnings.
- A high-tech organization emerging from venture capital support found its "President's Club" sales people (i.e., the top sellers) were more confident with a new solution-selling strategy, demonstrating its effectiveness.

Yet they could also more easily pinpoint sales-support lapses that could derail the new approaches.

- Contrary to common wisdom among human-resource professionals, employee engagement is not the best indicator of future customer loyalty and re-purchase behavior. In fact, in scientific head-to-head tests,[3] the best predictor of customer loyalty is service climate (preparation, support, and recognition for being focused on the customer).

These are all examples of organization-specific research aimed at understanding how the available evidence—measurable indicators in particular—can predict Future Performance. Moving beyond generic findings discovered to work in other organizations, research done locally will help organizations converge on the most important ways to conceptualize Current Performance and focus on the shortlist of most potent indicators.

The focus of this research section has been on indicators and evaluations of Current Performance and not of Future Potential. The next section will explain why the qualities of unique transformations or unprecedented breakthroughs defy traditional measurement and research.

Future Potential Indicators

The biggest mistake people make is measuring Future Potential or exploration efforts with Current Performance or execution metrics, such as budget or length of time. Think about those ants from the beginning of this chapter: You cannot judge the pioneer ants by the time it takes them to develop a new path to food, just as workplace explorers should not be judged by the time it takes them to make a major organizational change.

As mentioned in previous chapters, most of an organization's energy will generally be spent on managing Current Performance. Future Potential will be focused on the "one thing" or "critical few" issues most important for achieving the strategic vision. That means that evaluating Future Potential will be more intensely focused on a smaller area of activity. This will be harder and quite possibly more important than evaluating Current Performance, because the future of the company depends upon it. Think again about those

[3] Brooks, S.M., Wiley, J.W., Hause, E.L., "Using Employee and Customer Perspectives to Improve Organizational Performance," *Customer Service Delivery: Research and Best Practices,* L. Fogli (ed.), (Jossey-Bass Publishers,) 52–82, 2006.

ants: If some follower ants slack off, the colony may go a little hungry but will not die, but if the pioneer ants fail to find new food sources, all the ants are in trouble.

The above discussion on Current Performance focused on ways to analyze existing data, generalizing it across settings to establish broad rules in order to predict future outcomes. Yet Future Potential efforts are often singular pursuits aimed at differentiating one's company from its competitors. Strategic uniqueness is at odds with scientific generalizability. There is a fundamental paradox in trying to measure the pursuit of breakthrough innovations, new service paradigms, or transformational leadership, because it is extremely difficult to measure the effectiveness of something that does not yet exist. If the nature of future approaches is so different from today's, there may be little hope to appropriately frame the right issues. If you already knew the question to ask and answer, this would not be a breakthrough innovation. As nuclear physicist Enrico Fermi explained, "If the result confirms the hypothesis, then you've made a measurement. If the result is contrary to the hypothesis, then you have made a discovery."

This does not mean that measuring breakthrough innovation is nothing more than a challenge: It is simply impossible. You cannot predict a specific future breakthrough with a well-grounded scientific model of organizational functioning. Science, by definition, is based on analysis of multiple cases that can generalize across contexts. Breakthroughs, on the other hand, are unique. Science may not be able to predict radical innovation, but can still guide companies—just not with precise prediction models. The next section will review some fundamental guidelines to help organizations better track and foster innovative activities. Just do not expect a single recipe for success. The evidence-based evaluation will be based on a broader array of information and weighted more toward the last three kinds of evidence listed at the beginning of this chapter—professional judgment, input of stakeholders, and intuition. This is not a liability to be lamented, but a reality to be embraced.

The Three Fundamentals of Future Potential Measurements

Measuring Future Potential requires a fundamentally different approach than measuring Current Performance, because building Future Potential is about risk, experimentation, and exploration of the unknown. Thus, typical metrics—such as ones dealing with cost or efficiency—will not work. In fact, these will be counterproductive and inhibit the need for creativity and play. Businesses are often advised to use the acronym "SMART" when outlining goals in order to define how they are **S**pecific, **M**easurable, **A**chievable, **R**elevant, and **T**ime-bound. While these are worthy characteristics to think through, especially for Current Performance goals, they are harder to apply to exploration into Future Potential, which defies specificity, requires adaptation to what's measurable, is less achievable the more audacious the breakthrough, and is still, it is hoped, relevant despite being difficult to predict. Similarly, any best practices, benchmarks, or other comparisons found outside of one's own organization are likely to be useless when measuring Future Potential. People want the comfort of established rules. But if you spend your precious Future Potential energies doing the same things that your competitors do, you will end up in an expensive arms race. The better pursuit is to capitalize on your own uniqueness and march off on your own into the unknown.

The second fundamental, then, is to evaluate which of your organization's competencies and work environments tend to give rise to new products, new approaches, or other radical changes. Regardless of the nature of the Future Potential that is being built, there are some ways to prepare. Investments can be measured; companies can evaluate what is needed to develop a new capability. Staffing projections can be made by focusing on the type of talent required to create and then implement a new approach. Organizational agility, resilience, and the overall climate for innovation are three aspects of an organization's culture that set the stage for exploration. See Fig. 7.1 for more on these concepts. The point of these different angles is that they help set the stage for exploration. They reflect having the right talent in place supported by the right investment, and the ability to experiment and play while still focusing on the core, strategic target.

The third fundamental is to increase the speed of learning from experience. Much of exploration is trying something until it fails, making adjustments, and trying something else. You may not be able to skip a step in this process, but you might be able to speed up your cycle time, and also maximize the learning from each time you try. Thomas Edison famously said, "I have not failed. I've just found 10,000 ways that won't work." To measure Edison's performance based on percentages of failures or some other form of efficiency would be ludicrous.

Learning a new skill is like building Future Potential. You are getting a baseline by identifying what comes easily versus not. Consider golf. If you are a fairly seasoned player (looking to streamline your Current Performance),

Agility
An organization is agile when it:
1. Actively and widely scans for new information about what is going on
2. Makes sense of ambiguous or uncertain situations
3. Is open to change
4. Takes advantage of opportunities quickly
5. Quickly deploys or redeploys resources to support execution

Resilience
An organization is resilient when it:
1. Has clearly defined and widely held values and beliefs
2. Has strong sense of identity and purpose that can survive anything
3. Has strong support network of external alliances or partnerships
4. Is expanding its external alliances and partnerships
5. Has "deep pockets;" access to capital and resources to weather anything

Innovation Climate
An organization has a climate to support innovation when employees:
1. Feel comfortable expressing new and innovative ways of doing things, including challenging conventional wisdom
2. Have time to develop new ideas
3. Believe the best ideas get the notice and sponsorship needed to move them forward
4. Are encouraged to take managed risks as long as we learn from them
5. Do a good job of testing new concepts and ideas in order to move ahead or "fail-fast"
6. Have the capacity (people, time, etc.) to act on promising new/innovative ideas

Fig. 7.1 Characteristics of organizational culture that promote building Future Potential

you can set a stroke target (a performance goal), based on the par for each hole (an external benchmark). If you are learning, you would do better to set a learning goal, such as working on how to putt better.

What do learning goals look like in the workplace? Assume you are the director of an R&D function, with a dozen projects underway. You expect at least 10 to fail. If you could talk to your one-year-into-the-future self to see what happened, you would jump at the chance. The drive to know which projects succeeded or failed is your biggest concern. If you could know faster, you and your team could make better use of resources, sales and marketing functions could more quickly adapt to emerging products, and operations could more effectively ramp up production. This is an extension of the "fail fast" concept. The faster you can figure out what does not work, the better— so long as you can learn from it and move on to something else.

As opposed to the efficiency measures of Current Performance, the focus on learning, and learning more quickly, will rightfully change your investments and energies regarding Future Potential. With golf, you might invest in a putting green in your backyard. With the dozen R&D projects, you might focus, like Edison, on refinements that increase the odds of the next being a success. Maybe you are chartered with expanding markets into China, or implementing a strategic selling approach. Learning from pursuits into new terrain is the number one goal, and should thus be reflected in evidence-based evaluations.

Keep these three fundamentals straight by thinking of an exploration expedition into the jungle. The first fundamental suggests that you do not measure progress hacking through the jungle the same way you would measure progress traveling back home. The second suggests that you know how to prepare for the unknown, with the right equipment and right people who have specialized skills. The third says that if you stumble onto a new kind of poisonous frog, or a ruin of an ancient civilization, or an impossible cliff, you will be able to adapt and respond.

Table 7.1 lists sample measures or other evidence to help contrast the differences between Current Performance and Future Potential. The Vitality Challenges

Table 7.1 Differences between evaluating Current Performance and Future Potential

Vitality challenge	Current Performance	Future Potential
Leadership	Revenue production, production output, meeting budget goals, or 360 or upward feedback scores	Leadership bench strength, 360 or upward feedback scores
Employees	Workforce competencies, employee engagement, safety record, voluntary turnover	Workforce analytics; climate for innovation, resilience, or adaptability
Processes	Resources per unit of production, customer delivery systems	Adaptability of production lines to new products
Offerings	Market share, comparisons to competitor products or services	Product pipeline, new markets, or revenue streams
Service	Service standards, up-selling and cross-selling performance	Service orientation of employees, or alignment of multiple service channels
Customers	Customer satisfaction with existing products or services, re-purchase rates, or switching costs	Customer relationships, brand image, sales pipeline within emerging markets, agility to move into new territories or segments

in the first column echo the challenges listed in Chap. 3. These are samples that would, of course, need to be matched to an organization's specific strategy.

The Balance of Performance and Potential

Once an organization has a grasp of how to evaluate Current Performance as well as Future Potential, the very real challenge remains of how to strike the right balance. Balance does not mean equal time devoted to each. As a starting point, assume that in any organization, 80% of time and resources are devoted to Current Performance, and 20% is spent to build Future Potential. But that can change. In a start-up organization, 100% is Future Potential. For bursts of time in a work group or business unit, it might be that "all hands on deck" are required to deliver current business needs without concern for the future. That would be 100% focus on Current Performance. The question of balance comes down to resources and investment. When do you spend more time and money on execution versus exploration? The answers will be a lot like balancing an investment portfolio, with some of the specifics depending on issues of portfolio maturity, tolerance for risk, time horizons for success, and so on. Like balancing an investment portfolio, the proper mix of Current Performance and Future Potential investments will change over time.

Revisiting the basic manufacturing example above will be helpful. One objective mentioned in the Current Performance section was to produce more units in less time. Another objective, based on a longer time horizon, would be to track the performance of this consumer product. Presumably once a new and fresh offering to the marketplace, this product has a lifespan that moves from heavy investment in the early years of the development stage, to profitability once execution has ramped up and the product has found its customer base, and eventually to shrinking margins as competitors enter the market, until it no longer makes sense to produce or support the product. By this time in the product lifecycle, the manufacturing organization hopes it has devoted enough product-development time to have a next-generation product launched before the previous generation dies.

Pharmaceutical companies, for example, have product cycles with very long time horizons. The product pipeline starts with a large number of drug possibilities developed in the lab, and, with each stage of exploration, the possibilities narrow through discovery and design, clinical trials, government approvals, and finally coming to market. This process can take more than a dozen years. After 20 years, drug patents typically expire (depending on the country), and generic versions come to market, turning the drugs into commodities. By reviewing the number of products at each stage of development, the company can evaluate its risk of stagnation. If no viable new drugs are in clinical trials, new sources of revenue will be limited. Over such a long timeframe, and with such specific milestones, rigorous plans can be made.

Most organizations, however, will not have the clarity of pharmaceutical companies. Product lifecycles are faster-paced or more chaotic. Some are on an annual schedule, such as automobile makers. Apple has a well-known annual cycle for iPhone generations, with more significant versions every two years. Retailers hawk the latest fashions every season. These companies have established rhythms for product exploration and manufacture. Oxbo, the harvesting company mentioned in Chap. 2, cycles its engineering energies between innovation in the off-season and product support during the harvest.

Not every industry has known schedules. Not all balancing concerns deal with product development. But it is clear that understanding your own cycles and rhythms matters. Research[4] has identified that being great at both Current Performance and Future Potential matters for financial success. Beyond that, particularly lopsided organizations, with extra strong effectiveness in Current Performance without commensurate focus and investment in Future Potential, actually have *worse* financial performance than those with weaker Current Performance, yet a more balanced approach. As expected, imbalance is rarely the result of overzealous exploration and focus on Future Potential, but of all-consuming execution and Current Potential that overrun investments in the future. This is exactly like an investment portfolio that is never rebalanced.

The rhythms of managing balance are different for different situations. How do you identify the rhythms that work for you? Whether you are leading a work group, a division, or an organization, there is a short list of steps to work through:

1. Identify from the Vitality Challenges those that are most important for the performance of your group and the pursuit of your strategy. (See Table 7.1 for sample evaluations, and Chap. 3 for a description of the challenges of and focus on strategy).

[4] Qing Cao, Gedajlovic E., Hongping Zhang, "Unpacking Organizational Ambidexterity: Dimensions, Contingencies, and Synergistic Effects," *Organization Science*, vol. 20, 781–796, 2009.

- Select the three that are most important for Current Performance.
- Select the one (*maybe* two) that most defines how you will be successful in the future.

2. Are there natural cycles to the challenges you selected? For example, leadership challenges may pivot around quarterly financial targets reflecting the Current Performance, to which leaders are accountable, as well as annual succession-planning process that fosters the Future Potential for the organization's leadership. There may be annual customer renewals for existing products, yet major product launches or grand openings or territory acquisitions are also planned. Or, there may be no natural cycles to either the Current Performance or Future Potential. Either way, map how exploration and innovation will transition into streamlined execution. Sometimes, artificial or imposed cycles are worthwhile, akin to making New Year's resolutions on December 31, even if there is no specific advantage to that time of year. Resolutions made at the New Year are up to 10 times more likely to be met than comparable resolutions made at other times of the year.[5]

3. As a thought experiment, interview your one-year-into-the-future self about these Challenges, probing with questions about these cycles: How will you have concluded that you are successful? What will you have learned? And where will you wish you would have invested more time and attention?

4. Specifically in regard to your pursuits: Where are Current Performance and Future Potential at odds with each other (e.g., the same people either deliver old products or invent new ones)? Where are they more synergistic (e.g., selling existing products is easier when customers know what is in your product pipeline)? And where do they literally compete for resources, and how easy is it to share or swap resources?

5. Ultimately, are you satisfied with your organization's ability to manage Current Performance? Are you satisfied with your organization's ability to build Future Potential?

Your answers to these questions will help to frame how to balance Current Performance with Future Potential, and more importantly, how you may need to adjust attention and investment.

[5] Norcross, J.C., Mrykalo, M.S., and Blagys, M.D., "Auld Lang Syne: Success predictors, change processes, and self-reported outcomes of New Year's resolvers and nonresolvers," *Journal of Clinical Psychology*, vol. 58, issue 4, 397–405, 2002.

Assessment: Evaluating Vitality

To determine how well you evaluate both your Current Performance and Future Potential efforts, evaluate the statements below. These first two are pass/fail prerequisite questions. Vital organizations should be able to clearly check off both of the two statements below before moving on:

- We have Current Performance evaluations that are metrics-oriented and based on factors such as efficiencies, speed, cost, or standardization. (These are not simply based on easily available data, but on carefully considered indicators of success.)
- We use a variety of evidence to determine progress in building Future Potential: We do NOT use efficiency, speed, cost, standardization, or long-term financial metrics to evaluate building Future Potential.

If you can agree with both of those prerequisite statements, then move to the next set. You should evaluate your organization or work group on the next three fundamentals regarding Future Potential:

- How we evaluate our Future Potential is unique to our situation. We do not use industry or other benchmarking to judge our progress.
- We evaluate how well we set the stage for breakthroughs in Future Potential (e.g., investments, agility, resilience, or innovation climate).
- We evaluate speed of learning (failing fast) or other specific learning goals with regard to Future Potential.

Finally, these last "advanced" items address how you manage your evaluations over time. These should be addressed after you have a solid foundation based on the fundamentals covered above:

- We evaluate our performance metrics to understand how they relate to outcome, and to refine the metrics accordingly.
- We review our metrics and accountabilities on a regular basis to ensure they support the original intent (and have not spawned mischief or counterproductive side-effects).
- We evaluate how well we eventually convert Future Potential exploration into Current Performance execution.

If you have the prerequisites covered, as well as the fundamentals, congratulations for being able to work on the advanced items. You are well on your way.

To take this and other assessments online, and get an interactive, customized report, visit OV-CVO.com.

CHAPTER 8

Navigating Change

Setting the Stage for Organizational Change

A large petrochemical company made a major leap toward building Future Potential by acquiring numerous organizations. This was a seismic change for the people employed at the different acquired companies around the globe. Often, in merger-and-acquisition situations, CEOs focus primarily on the financials of the companies, which include the mix of products that can be offered, the enhanced footprint, and the customer base. They often take steps such as reducing production, labor, and overhead costs by eliminating redundancy and streamlining. But in this particular case, the Vitality-oriented CEO understood the potential that could be achieved by combining and retaining the best talent within the component organizations, as long as the mergers successfully integrated the different cultures. He implemented a strategy that was unique to his company and particular situation, differentiating his organization in the highly competitive petrochemical industry. He communicated his vision for the future, and then backed it up with solid actions to show his employees that he was serious. He made sure to utilize top talent from the different organizations, taking care that the plum jobs didn't all go to employees from the original company. The goal was to have all employees, regardless of their heritage, feel as though their roles were integral to the company's long-term success, that they personally had a positive future and long-term career potential with the emergent organization, and that they would be given the tools needed to help the company achieve its goals. This effort took time, but over a two-year period the separate organizations successfully merged into one united company.

Message, Performance, and Future: An Approach to Transformation

How was the CEO so successful despite such a difficult task? He managed to use three key tools that are fundamental to effecting change in any major organization: Message, Performance, and Future. (See Fig. 8.1).

The Message focuses on sharing the rationale and motivation driving the change, and explaining employees' roles during and after the transition. The Performance piece involves making sure that employees are given the tools they need to carry out their tasks. Finally, Future refers to illustrating to employees both the company's long-term Future Potential and their own individual ability to thrive within the organization. When all three pieces are in place—the Message, Performance, and Future—employees are more likely to support the change and feel motivated to contribute to its success.

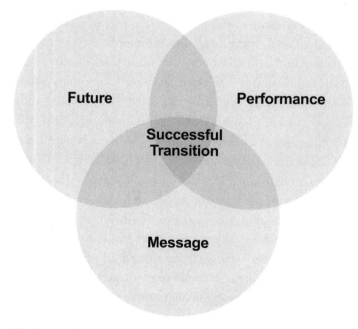

Fig. 8.1   Fundamental issues of change

In the case of the petrochemical company, the CEO helped his company and employees successfully navigate change by sharing his vision and describing the organization's increased capabilities (the Message), specifically spending a great deal of effort showcasing the additional strength and opportunities of the combined companies. Additionally, the CEO took the best processes from each of the respective organizations, seamlessly integrating them (the Performance). He also made sure that the best employees were given appropriate positions regardless of which company they had come from. Once this state was set, the credibility and clarity of the overall direction and support naturally generated an excitement among the members of the workforce about what the future may hold for both themselves and the organization in regards to exploration and Future Potential (the Future).

You need Message, Performance, and Future to navigate transitions smoothly. Sometimes, companies only manage to communicate or implement two out of the three circles from Fig. 8.1. If the Message and Performance pieces are there, but not the Future, employees will know what they need to do and be given the tools needed, but will not feel any obligation or commitment to the company. Employees may be disinterested in or disengaged from their work. Customers will experience that disinterest. When the Performance and Future aspects are present, but not Message, employees may be uncertain about what they are working on, and final products or goals are often unclear. Priorities will continually change. Customers will often experience the uncertainty in these situations as uneven service, product quality, or attractiveness. Finally, companies that share a Future and Message without Performance are offering employees goals and a vision, as well as a great deal of work, but not the tools to get that work done. In these companies, workload is often exceedingly high, as people struggle with ineffective processes, and top leadership is often viewed as weak or ineffective.

To ensure that your company is meeting Message, Performance, and Future, first identify every individual or group affected by the change. Identify key influencers, especially those who need to be onboard because of their ability to influence others. Make sure the Message is accepted by the employees involved, and then determine the Performance level of each group by taking stock of its ability and readiness to manage the change. Finally, make sure employees are confident in the organization's future, and their own.

Rhythms of Change

Change is part of the underlying rhythm within the vital organization. The changes that are made to streamline Current Performance may involve scaling production, driving consistency into service delivery, or streamlining costs, all of which generally have established cycles or timeframes. Future Potential must eventually encompass change that enables less well-known exploration, and the ultimate evolution from that exploration into Current Performance execution. Remember Levi Strauss from Chap. 5? He not only invented blue jeans, but also changed his company to manufacture them at scale and bring them to market with a distribution system that let him maximize profits. You must continue to develop new products or services, bring them to market in order to generate performance and, as a result, more revenue, which enables your organization to continue its exploration. Throughout these repetitive cycles, your company's overarching and compelling vision will help you—and all employees—navigate these changes without losing focus on the bigger picture.

In vital organizations, it's possible that change is geared toward either maintaining Current Performance or—a greater challenge—to building Future Potential. This can cause its own problems, as employees tasked with the side of the business not driving the change (or reaping its rewards) may have a harder time acclimating to it. Leaders can minimize this possibility by ensuring that the Message is shared specifically with those employees, and includes a discussion on how these employees and their areas of focus will also benefit.

Incremental Versus Dramatic Change

Stagnation is not an option for any company that wants to survive. But as leaders create the necessary modifications within their organizations—whether they are changes made to help maintain or enhance Current Performance or to build Future Potential—they must implement the correct degree of change over the proper time period. When is it appropriate for an organization to take a more incremental approach, changing slowly over time, and when is more rapid, dramatic change necessary? The answer depends once again on both your organization and the specific issue at hand. There are certain issues in organizations that require gradual shifts, bringing the entire organization up to speed over a long period of time, and then there are other changes that are much more likely to be beneficial if they are done dramatically and rapidly, providing a clear break with the ways things were done in the past. As you would expect, maintaining Current Performance usually entails smaller, more adaptable changes, while building Future Potential frequently requires bigger, more dramatic changes that involve more work to ensure a smooth transition.

Incremental change is appropriate when a company's vision and strategy are aligned, when performance is acceptable, and when the future looks solid, but the company nevertheless needs to evolve to adapt to a changing environment. However, if the managers of an organization desire to reach a breakthrough—the Future Potential—they will need a new strategy that requires dramatic change.

An organization also needs to make a dramatic shift in strategy if the leaders decide it is the wrong strategy for achieving Future Potential. Dramatic change should be the order of the day when disruptive forces enter your market, when economic conditions push your organization to the edge, or when a fundamental change is necessary to build the future.

By definition, if the vision and strategy are wrong for the times, the organization is doing the wrong things, and it is time for immediate change. Here is an extreme example: After the terrorist hijackings on 9/11, some federal law-enforcement agencies immediately had to change their missions and strategies to deal with this type of threat. It was no longer about catching criminals and building cases against them after the fact, but rather deterrence in order to prevent these acts from occurring in the first place. This required a dramatic shift in tactics and the skill sets needed among employees.

Framework for Determining Incremental or Dramatic Change

You know you need to make a change. The question is: Do you plunge right in, or move more slowly? Realistically, most organizational shifts require elements that incorporate both incremental and dramatic changes. Think about two companies that merge: Changes to the brand identity may be made slowly to acclimate customers over time, but the organizational structure will change greatly and quickly. While every situation is unique, change made to maintain Current Performance is usually incremental, but may, at times, require more dramatic shifts. Future Potential efforts usually require major dramatic changes. To help guide your change-related actions, see Table 8.1, which sets forth a framework for determining when an organization should effect incremental or dramatic change.

Table 8.1 Incremental versus dramatic change

	Make dramatic changes if:	Make incremental changes if:
Company message and strategy are clear and sound	Employees are confused about what the organization stands for and their role in accomplishing the goals	The organization needs to improve on their core business practices
Policies, practices, and procedures are supportive of fundamental messages	The policies, practices, and procedures contradict or do not reward what the organization stands for	The organization rewards the behaviors it wants employees to exhibit
People feel like they have a future within the organization	Morale is low, turnover is high, and performance needs improvement	People feel good about where the organization is going and where they are going within the organization
General performance of the organization on critical daily elements	Processes are broken	Processes are working well
Competitive environment	Rapid change is required to stay competitive	Environment is relatively stable
Economic conditions	Rapidly changing	Stable economic environments
Expansion plans	Expanding into new markets or developing/ introducing new products or services	Small changes may be needed as part of larger changes
Mergers and acquisitions	You are consolidating redundant capabilities	Strong brand and customer recognition of acquired products and services
Zero-tolerance items	The issue is about ethics, safety, sexual harassment, etc.	

Incremental Versus Dramatic Change: A Story

Think for a minute of two organizations (Company Big Box and Company Clean 'N Neat) where the maximization of customer-service performance is critical. Each of these organizations has 500 retail outlet locations. Big Box scores 40% favorability on a measure of customer service, while Clean 'N Neat scores 65%. If you were to examine the distribution of scores across each of the 500 retails stores for both of these organizations, you would likely find a normal distribution, with the bulk of stores operating around average, but some stores performing either below or above average. Both companies desire to improve their score on customer focus as part of their strategies to achieve their goals.

There are at least three ways for both of these organizations to improve. First, they could ask every retail outlet to improve their score by three points, moving Big Box to 43% and Clean 'N Neat to 68%. This is a shift in the entire distribution, improving the scores of all 500 stores. Alternatively, they could focus on the bottom 10–15% of stores and design a strategy to bring them up to average, reducing the variance and increasing the consistency of the customer experience between stores. This method often makes sense in today's climate of reducing headcount and doing more with less, where it is often helpful to target your intervention to the bottom performers rather than trying for a broad change effort that may fail due to a lack of resources. A targeted intervention can also have more of an impact on the total distribution—the average scores across all the stores—than trying to move the total distribution. Finally, a third path to change is to set an improvement target across all the stores while at the same time working with the low-end outliers to bring their scores up at least to average.

If you were the CEO of Company Big Box or Clean 'N Neat, which path would you choose?

The answer depends on the current score of the company. Clean 'N Neat, with a fairly high score of 65%, would benefit from setting improvement targets and working with the bottom end of the distribution, because their customer service-oriented strategy is working well. Change for Clean 'N Neat can be incremental. But Big Box, with a much lower score, should go for dramatic change, because it has a much larger leap to make. It doesn't have the time to make incremental changes. There is something broken at Big Box, potentially something fundamental, which is affecting its Current

Performance and overall Vitality. It could be process-oriented, it could be cultural, or it could be poor leadership, but something is not working and dramatic things need to happen to fix it.

In either case, dramatic or incremental change can cause discomfort for those who must live through it. Clearly, dramatic change often causes greater discomfort. A merger or re-organization often results in intense changes to the organization, causing anxiety and stress to employees. To alleviate this, it is important to give people as much control over their personal circumstances as possible. Additionally, support from the organization as they navigate the changes will help as well. Try and make the change meaningful to your employees, both in terms of the work they do for the company as well as how it impacts them personally. Again, make sure you are focused on the three aspects of navigating change: Message, Performance, and Future.

The story of Big Box and Clean 'N Neat may give you a simplified example of how executives may be triggered to act. The need for change will not always be a clear-cut as it shown here; sometimes the change may be less tangible, as when an organization is looking to make a paradigm shift. Furthermore, implementing real, lasting, and overall change often encompasses many smaller changes, which can be either incremental or dramatic, or a combination of both. When implementing change, the line upward may not always be straight, but it is nonetheless an important path to travel on the journey toward Vitality.

Changing Behaviors and Attitudes

Getting employees to accept and support change can be a challenge. Even when the Message, Performance, and Future pieces are in place, there may be push-back from some individuals. People's behaviors and attitudes are often so deeply ingrained that they may be reluctant to shift their behavior, even when the directive comes from the top leadership level. Employees will be hesitant to make any behavioral or attitude shifts if they perceive any loss to their own personal situation. Furthermore, employees rarely just take the word of senior executives; they need to see decisive action surrounding the change in order to start abiding by it.

So what do companies need to do in order to change both behaviors and attitudes? The answer is a tricky chicken-or-the-egg quandary. Companies will not be able to change attitudes without changing behaviors, but it can be difficult to change behaviors when employee attitudes are so ingrained. While it is important to work on both attitudes and behaviors simultaneously, it is usually easier to start with employee behaviors: Enable people to make the necessary changes by giving them both the rationale behind the change and the tools they need to implement it.

One large agribusiness commissioned a study to monitor employees' attitudes regarding quality while they implemented a Six-Sigma process improvement strategy and trained employees on quality, as well as modified their manufacturing methods and utilized techniques such as Xbar and R charting. Leaders felt certain that the new techniques would lead to fewer defects per million parts manufactured, and would also lead to increases in employee perceptions toward the quality of the product. For a while they were correct: The surveys, which were done every six months for two years, showed improvements in perceptions of quality that corresponded to the actual number of defects. As the number of defects went down, the perception of quality improved. However, eventually higher employee standards towards quality emerged and perceptions shifted downward, even as the number of defects continued to go down. Attitudes regarding what was acceptable had shifted upwards and the previously set quality goals were no longer high enough. This was viewed as a victory, as it demonstrated that, by changing behaviors around quality, attitudes towards quality could be shifted as well.

Helping Employees Cope with Dramatic Change

In general, and especially in times of change, it is important to provide employees with a sense of control, in whatever fashion and to whatever extent that you can, in order to improve their ability to cope with emotions and the thought patterns that often accompany dramatic change. A merger, a re-organization, a change in responsibilities, or a new boss can result in uncertainties that cause employees substantial stress or anxiety. Empowering employees during these times will mitigate that. Given the varying nature of how individuals react to stress, you will not be entirely successful, but it is in both the employees' and organization's best interests to assist them as much as possible.

An approach used by some when managing employees is to promote regular ongoing change for the sake of change itself, to foster uncertainty—to keep an organization somewhat chaotic and in a constant state of upheaval.

This approach proposes that fostering a state of uncertainty by, for example, often reorganizing or changing processes and otherwise keeping the organization in flux, will keep the organization nimble and on its toes, and will spur innovation. This is not goal-driven re-organization or change that is tied to the implementation of a specific strategy, but rather done for the sake of the perceived benefits of change and upheaval. In other words, it is done for artificial and ill-conceived reasons. When applied, this approach rarely if ever works the way it is intended. Chaos is just that—chaos. Most people, including both your employees and customers, have a tremendous need for consistency. To the extent that people are living and dealing with a chaotic environment, stress will greatly increase and the performance you will get out of people will decrease.

Catalysts for Change

Though consistency generally improves performance, strategic periods of chaos can be catalysts for transformative innovation. Importantly, this is chaos as a side-effect of transformation, not chaos pursued to keep things edgy. Kurt Lewin's well-known change management model[1] uses the notion of unfreezing, changing, and then re-freezing the organization in order to enable change. An unfreezing event, whether at the organizational level or individual level, is a paradigm-shifting event that is significant enough that it enables change to occur. It is the notion that a "burning platform" is essential for motivating change—especially dramatic change needed to drive the "Big I" innovation discussed in Chap. 6, or the changes needed to build Future Potential. Nothing can prompt significant changes in habits like a life-changing event. The unfreezing allows for the change, then you want to re-freeze around the new behaviors or processes in order to turn them into Current Performance. However, if leaders artificially induce chaos without communicating a compelling vision for the future—a Message—the results could be disastrous. Leaders cannot be lazy. Define and craft a vision with the right metrics and the right vision to induce people forward.

Stephen Jay Gould created a concept within the world of evolutionary biology called punctuated equilibrium. The notion is that things are stable as they move along the evolutionary track, but then there are bursts of very

---

[1] Burnes, B., "Kurt Levin and the Planned Approach to Change: A Re-appraisal," *Journal of Management Studies* 41:6, September 2004.

rapid and dramatic change over a short period of time. This burst of rapid change may be due to animals having to deal with rapidly changing environmental conditions. It does not take much of a stretch of the imagination to think of organizational change from this perspective as well. The organization remains fairly stable until something in its environment unfreezes it and forces a burst of rapid change. The argument is that stabilizing around the new behaviors, operating methods, or culture brought about by the change is useful and prevents the organization from feeling like it is always in a permanent state of chaos and change.

Legislating Change

In 1964, the US Civil Rights Act came into being, signed into law by President Lyndon B. Johnson. The purpose of the law was to make discrimination based on race, religion, color, national origin, and gender illegal. Beyond simply making discrimination illegal, the legislation was attempting a feat of social engineering by changing behavior. And while one could argue that tremendous strides have been made, make no mistake about it, there is still plenty of discrimination going on today.

Can an organization, in this case the US Federal Government, issue orders and simply expect people to fall in line? Does legislation and prosecution for violations of that legislation create morality, or is it only an illusion of morality?

While we could argue endlessly whose standards of morality, or which cultures and norms we will accept as "moral," it is clear that legislation does have the power to affect behaviors, and that over time thought patterns can be altered. Perhaps not for everyone, and not in every instance, but changing behaviors can lead to attitudinal shifts in a large population.

The attempt to legislate behavior is nothing new, as there were many ancient legal codes aimed at instructing people how to live their lives in an attempt to instill order in society. One well-known early attempt at legislating morality occurred under the Babylonian ruler Hammurabi about 3800 years ago. The Code of Hammurabi consisted of 282 laws by which people were expected to live their lives. Hammurabi's code was the source of the saying "an eye for an eye." ("If a man put out the eye of another man, his eye shall be put out.") And it is likely the earliest instance of medical reimbursement legislation. ("If a physician make a large incision with an operating knife and cure it, or if he open a tumor [over the eye] with an operating knife, and saves the eye, he shall receive ten shekels in money.") But medical malpractice carried stiff penalties under Hammurabi. ("If a physician make a large incision with the operating knife, and kill him, or open a tumor with the operating knife, and cut out the eye, his hands shall be cut off.")

An even older set of laws, originating about 300 years before Hammurabi, was created by the King of Ur and called the code of Ur-Nammu. Some of those very ancient laws we would recognize today. ("If a man commits a murder, that man must be killed.") And some would be somewhat foreign to us today. ("If a man is accused of sorcery he must undergo ordeal by water; if he is proven innocent, his accuser must pay three shekels.")

Almost 1000 years later, Moses brought down a set of laws from Mount Sinai which also was aimed at describing to people how they were expected to behave and live their lives (e.g. "You shall not murder").

While there were certainly differences among these legal codes, there were also some very interesting similarities. For instance look across these four sets of moral codes, originating thousands of years apart, regarding what they have to say about bearing false witness:

- Ur-Nammu (4100 years ago)—"If a man appeared as a witness, and was shown to be a perjurer, he must pay fifteen shekels of silver."
- Hammurabi (3800 years ago)—"If any one bring an accusation of any crime before the elders, and does not prove what he has charged, he shall, if it be a capital offense charged, be put to death."
- Moses (approx. 3000 years ago)—"You shall not bear false witness against your neighbor."
- And today in the USA (18 U.S. Code § 1621) perjury is still a crime—"... is guilty of perjury and shall, except as otherwise expressly provided by law, be fined under this title or imprisoned not more than five years, or both."

Apparently bearing false witness has been an on-going problem since the dawn of civilization, or there would have been no need to call it out specifically in each of these moral codes.

More recently, the case for legislating morality can be seen with the advent of laws in favor of marriage equality and other equal benefits for the LGBTQ community. In this particular case, it seems that the attitudes of the population in general were ahead, and perhaps still are ahead, of those in various legislative bodies in the USA. There are of course segments of the population who vehemently oppose equal rights, just as there were those who supported Jim Crow laws in the South. What will likely happen to that group over time? As LGBTQ rights become more widespread, and people or states are held accountable for violations of those rights, the act of behaving in a fashion supportive of those rights will be seen as *normal*—people will want to be similar, including in attitude, to the vast majority of people they are surrounded by. In other words, "People will maintain a belief in a position when surround by a community of like-minded believers."[2]

And again, potentially not everyone's beliefs will positively shift in every instance (even among those suffering from cognitive dissonance), but across the larger population, continuing shifts in attitudes could be measured.

Legislating morality and behavior change to establish a culture is possible in societies and organizations, but over the long term, true shifts in attitudes will only happen if they are supported by corresponding behaviors.

Assessment: Navigating Change

Change is clearly instrumental in the pursuit of Vitality. Without it, there could be no Future Potential, and certainly no cycle from Future Potential into Current Performance. For each of the statements below, check the items that reflect the reality of your organization:

- We have a clear change agenda as it relates to streamlining Current Performance (i.e., improving the ways we execute).
- We have a focused change agenda as it relates to building Future Potential (i.e., the exploration and transformation we will invest in to remain a vital organization).
- The Message of changes we undertake is clear and disseminated; we have a shared vocabulary and frequent dialog across the organization for talking about change, improvements, and innovation. In other words, we know what we mean when we talk about such change.
- The Performance demands based on the changes being implemented are met and provided for, the implications of changes we undertake are clear and addressed, and employees have the tools and resources they need to succeed in changed environment.
- The Future roles of individuals and of the changes we undertake are clear; there is a confidence in our ability to manage the change, and employees understand what change means for them personally and how they will fit into new environment.

[2] Kahneman, D., and Tversky, A. "Judgement Under Certainty: Heuristics and Biases," *Science*, v. 185 no 4157, 1124–1131, 1974.

Endorsing all five items would be spectacular. Envisioning and clearly articulating the need to change is very difficult, let alone providing the resources to make it happen. The first two reflect the underlying business need, and the last three reflect your discipline in change management.

To take this and other assessments online, and get an interactive, customized report, visit OV-CVO.com.

CHAPTER 9

Making Change Stick

New Year's Resolutions

It is a common dilemma. You know where you need to improve. You believe that it is a worthy effort. You *want* to improve. But life gets in the way. You often do not live up to your own ambitions.

In the United States, roughly half of all adults make New Year's resolutions—a commitment at the start of the calendar year to make some sort of self-improvement. Typical goals focus on losing weight, quitting smoking, managing money better, or being more organized. They represent our ambitions to become the individuals we want to be. Some represent doing existing things better, such as reducing debt faster, while some represent more fundamental changes in how we live, such as starting one's own business.

But how many people are actually successful? While research estimates vary, success rates might be just shy of 50% after six months, but drop to closer to 20% two years later. That might sound depressing, given that most resolutions fail to sustain improvement. But from another angle, change is *hard*. A fifty-fifty chance at some sort of meaningful improvement after six months of some significant self-improvement, and a one in five shot after two years, sounds like something worth understanding a little better. In fact, resolutions made at New Year's are up to ten times more effective than comparable commitments made at other times of the year.[1]

---

[1] Norcross, J., Ph.D, *Changeology: 5 Steps to Realizing your Goals and Resolutions.* (New York: Simon & Schuster, 2012.)

While there are differences, certainly, between personal New Year's resolutions and organizational efforts to improve performance, there are three important lessons of successful resolutions that help guide organizational change, and the effort to live up to the goals one has already set.

First, resolutions need to be social. Part of the success of resolutions made at New Year's versus other times of the year is that there is a collective understanding—and corresponding support—for self-improvement. Additionally, including a buddy in one's resolutions can dramatically improve success. Studies show that something as simple as texting a buddy when you take an action toward your goal triples the rate of success.[2]

Second, rhythms matter. Annually revisiting aspirations, recalibrating, and setting goals for improvement is a rhythm that fits how we think and act in our lives. Seasons, birthdays, holidays, and other anniversaries all add punctuation to how we plan for and evaluate personal progress. Comparable rhythms hold within organizations with revenue reporting, seasonal booms and busts, product-release schedules, and strategic planning.

Third, the most successful resolutions are opportunities to "connect with your ideal self," according to Stanford professor Kelly McGonigal in *The Willpower Instinct*. Like an organization's efforts to execute on its strategy, New Year's resolutions for self-improvement offer an opportunity to reflect on who you really want to be, and to invest in that goal.

Resolutions for Organizational Change

How does the struggle of New Year's resolutions translate into organizational change? Deciding what to change and enlisting the buy-in of employees is difficult enough. This is the setting and clarifying of resolutions, as discussed in the previous chapter. Real change requires executives, managers, and employees to change behavior, not just for a while, but permanently. Much of the failure to change is not based on poor decisions about direction or lack of initial enthusiasm, but failure to follow through. An organization's resolutions to improve need special attention and support, helping employees manage through the uncertainties of new approaches until they become "normal."

Importantly, not all kinds of change efforts are equal. In the language of Vitality, the two types of organizational change are about improving the

[2] Parker, C., "New Year's Resolutions that Connect with the 'Ideal Self' Are Most Effective, Stanford Psychologist Says," *Stanford News*, January 2015.

efficiency of Current Performance and finding new ways to create Future Potential. Improving Current Performance involves making incremental changes to the things that an organization already does, such as faster manufacture of widgets, better access to sales information to support new clients, or more consistency in service models within a product line. This kind of change is like a New Year's Resolution to do what you already do, like to run a mile with a faster time or to lose 10 pounds. While not easy, these changes are more predictable, more easily planned, and more effectively supported than efforts to build Future Potential.

The breakthrough or paradigm-busting changes that are a part of Future Potential tend to be much more mysterious. These involve inventing new products, penetrating new markets, or building new capabilities. These kinds of changes are more directly connected to an organization's (or work unit's) strategies. They resemble New Year's resolutions that are harder to quantify, and press into uncharted terrain, such as learning a new skill or traveling to a foreign country. An organization's efforts to build Future Potential are harder to predict with regard to timelines or cost, more difficult to plan, and require extra organizational support. Building Future Potential requires more clarity, commitment, and discipline.

Living Up to Intentions to Change

We need to recognize the psychological dilemma that good intentions do not automatically lead to change. Day-to-day realities often impede our ability to realize our vision of transformation. However, there are different avenues we can pursue that help us live up to our own good intentions to change and hold ourselves, or our employees, accountable to expectations.

Clear Goals

The direction or target for change needs to be clearly defined. It has to be acknowledged, if not embraced, by all employees actively involved in the change process. It has been shown over and over again that specific and challenging yet achievable goals produce greater performance results than simple "do your best" goals.[3] Reducing accidents or production defects in a manufacturing facility can

---

[3] Locke, E.A., Latham, G.P., "New Directions in Goal-Setting Theory," *Current Directions in Psychological Science* 15 (5): 265–268, October 2006.

be a clear goal, potentially expressed in a metric. These kinds of goals would be about streamlining Current Performance, and will be among the easiest to define. Developing sufficient, innovative enhancements in time for next year's product release might be a fully embraced goal, in the sense that everyone might accept the basic need as well as the deadline. This kind of building Future Potential goal can be articulated with a certain amount of clarity (see Chap. 7 on evaluating Vitality). However, the exact nature of the innovations may not become known until the work is well underway. The nature of Future Performance goals requires leaders to save room for working with and around initial intuitions, suddenly inspired left turns, and technical challenges. Following from the discussion in Chap. 7, while you cannot hold people accountable to cost and time metrics when building Future Potential, you can at least hold them accountable for learning something, such as what might work, what will not, or competencies required for new activities. For example, if you are expanding into China, the accountability might not be a sales target, but at least one big, strategically relevant deal that demonstrates understanding and executing against the new demands of that market. If you are developing a new product, the accountability might be to have a clearly articulated story for the next consumer conference. If you are transforming service approaches with new technology, the goal might be converting a major client to the new platform and developing a list of hotspots for converting others. There are many ways to create accountabilities that maximize the progress made with Future Performance efforts. The keys are to stay flexible and to keep an eye on how you will convert those breakthrough innovations into streamlined execution in the future.

Keep in mind that to achieve the kind of clarity needed to hold people accountable requires a high degree of collegial agreement on whether the goals were accomplished or not. It is critical, however, that the need for clarity does not overwhelm the essence of the goal. Goals that are more vaguely defined but closer to the target are better than crystal-clear goals that are off-target. This will be more of a risk in defining goals related to Future Potential.

Tracking Progress

Once you have a goal, and an agreed-upon way to know if it will be accomplished or not, the next step is to develop a tracking approach to make sure you stay on the right path. Here are a couple of key points about tracking. First, besides the more mechanical side of enabling adjustments to plans, resources, and approaches, tracking provides motivation for people. Think of those thermometer graphs favored by fundraising groups, which show their progress up the thermometer as they raise money. Other companies may post numbers of days without an accident. These work because people like a visual aid that shows them how close the finish line is, or how far they have come in a streak. In fact, according to Google, health-and-fitness apps topped their list of fastest-growing categories in the Play Store in 2014,[4] because people use them to track their individual performance. Second, tracking should be made public. Being social, creating buddy systems, or enabling a buzz across a workplace makes a difference. This adds drive and support for finishing. Many of those health-and-fitness apps allow you to post your workout results or weight-loss achievements on Facebook or Twitter to share with your social network. Of course, within organizations, there may be limitations to public tracking efforts. Some kinds of accountabilities may relate to personally sensitive issues (such as 360 feedback results), and some may be organizationally confidential (such as Future Potential efforts related to competitive strategy). But whatever is being tracked, consider making it as public as possible.

Perceived Consequences

Tracking is a good start for motivating people, but you can add some teeth to the effort by adding either positive or negative consequences, or rewards or punishments. Consequences can also be public, because people are often motivated by others knowing about their performances, but do not necessarily need to be. Examples of consequences include incorporating progress evaluations into performance appraisals, having to provide quarterly updates to executives, tying bonuses or other rewards explicitly to demonstrated improvements, or other kinds of recognition for success. Specifics will depend on the nature of the improvements—or resolutions—being pursued. In general, consequences should be fair and commensurate with the work being done. They must communicate the value-fit to organizational objectives, be meaningful to employees, and must be well-known and documented at the outset of the goal period. Finally, positive consequences should be achievable by the individuals or teams being tracked.

---

[4] Boxall, A., "2014 Is the Year of Health and Fitness Apps, Says Google," *Digital Trends*, December 2014.

Nudges

The accountability approaches described above are very logical and often methodical, and suggest a fairly straightforward change-management plan. This might be sufficient if all change and all people were always logical, methodical, and straightforward, but that is clearly not the case. Nudges, as described in *Nudge: Improving Decisions About Health, Wealth, and Happiness* by Richard Thaler and Cass Sunstein,[5] are generally simple ways to structure choices that do not force us into a specific action, but rather help guide us toward better options. Rather than ignoring or lamenting our human foibles, nudges are based on research in psychology and behavioral economics, and work with cognitive biases and emotional tendencies. In describing these foibles, Thaler and Sunstein assert, "The picture that emerges is one of busy people trying to cope in a complex world in which they cannot afford to think deeply about every choice they have to make." In other words, people make bad choices because they don't have the time, energy, capacity, or ability to make thoughtful decisions. To help us live better, examples of nudges include putting the carrots at eye level in a cafeteria line and the chocolate around the corner, making 401k investment options default to an age-appropriate mutual fund (while still offering a potentially paralyzing array of other choices), or making organ-donation decisions "opt-out" instead "opt-in." In these examples, people are still making their own choices. They are not being forced to do anything they do not want to do. However, they are generally being guided toward better behaviors, whether those behaviors benefit the individual, organization, or society at large. Situations where nudges help are often those where costs and benefits are separated in time. These are situations where there are costs now and benefits later (like saving for retirement or making the time to exercise), where individuals are less likely to engage in these behaviors because the pay-off comes much later. Alternatively, they may be situations where there are benefits now and costs later (like eating chocolate cake or smoking), where we are more likely to engage in what we know we should not do because the consequences come much later.

In the workplace, the efforts to make improvements to Current Performance and Future Potential are certainly candidates for nudging. Nudges are most useful when: Individuals are inexperienced or poorly informed; the tasks are

[5] Thaler, R., and Sustein, C., *Nudge: Improving Decisions about Health, Wealth, and Happiness.* (New York: Penguin Books, 2009).

difficult, rare, or unfamiliar; feedback is slow or infrequent; and it is hard to know what "good" looks like. If you have ever said something like, "I really should devote more time to X," then you have encountered a situation ripe for nudging.

Below are some examples of kinds of nudges, and how they might play out in helping to streamline Current Performance or build Future Potential:

- **Commitment devices**. This is when you make a commitment today to ensure you fulfill it tomorrow. There are alarm clocks that, if you do not get up on time, will shred money you inserted the night before or send embarrassing tweets that you set up. In the workplace, an employee might schedule a conference or other presentation on a topic not yet fully explored in order to create the pressure to be compelling in front of peers. The trick with commitment devices is to make sure that, as you or your employees adapt to them, you change them accordingly to keep them effective.

- **Social Norms/Pressure**. This is not an artificial "peer pressure" notion from junior high school, but rather a message about what is acceptable behavior, which can be welcome information, especially in unfamiliar situations. Consider that the plea not to take petrified wood samples from the Petrified Forest National Park, because too many people do it: This actually backfires because most people assume that because so many people do it, it is acceptable behavior and they will miss out on getting a sample otherwise. At work, laments about only having time to run from meeting to meeting will similarly send the wrong message. As Thaler and Sunstein suggest, "If you want to nudge people into socially desirable behavior, do not, by any means, let them know that their current actions are better than the social norm." Instead, reinforce the idea that other people spend time on improvement. At your organization, you can do this by emphasizing the idea that it is the social norm to set aside time to dream about either "Big I" or "Little i" innovation. Promoting social norms cannot be too artificial, but you can make it easier for positive stories to be re-told and harder for negative stories to be heard.

- **Change defaults**. A default is what happens when you take no action. This is the path of least resistance. Setting up automatic payments to a retirement account, rather than having to write checks each month, is an example of changing a default to help you live up to a resolution to save more for retirement. The nudge of changing defaults is about changing what happens when people do nothing. The organ-donation or voter-registration forms that ask you to "opt-out" (i.e., select *not* to do it) as opposed to asking you to "opt-in" (i.e., select to do it) are a clear example. At work, with regard to how you attend to Current Performance and Future Potential, ask yourself, "What are the defaults? Where do people spend time and energy as a part of the day-to-day?" Evaluate if your answers match your ideal, and if needed, change the defaults in how people spend time, how they allocate resources, how they communicate progress, and so on.

- **Framing**. An underlying theme of this book deals with how an organization's pursuits are communicated. In general, Vitality, strategy, and change efforts all have a frame around them. The job of leaders is to help define that frame, and not simply to allow employees to create their own version. Framing as a nudge refers to managing the psychological descriptions of risks of gain versus loss. People typically hate losing something more than they like winning that same thing. As Thaler and Sunstein assert, "Roughly speaking, losing something makes you twice as miserable as gaining the same thing makes you happy." People are more likely to engage in self-examinations for skin and breast cancer if they are told about the increased risk if they fail to do so, as opposed to being told about the reduced risk if they conduct the self-examinations. That may sound confusing, as though it were merely an issue of semantics, but that is not the case. Now, consider the fact that most breakthrough innovation efforts will fail. Match that with the notion that without any breakthroughs, an organization will eventually become obsolete. How should these risks—and opportunities—be framed? First, you will need to counteract the fear of failure for any one innovation attempt. You do not want to freeze people out of taking those risks. Instead, risks are required on the path to success. Second, you want to make clear the risk of not achieving any breakthroughs. Without overstating, the risk of ultimate organizational obsolescence should not be swept under the rug.
- **Priming**. A simple version of priming is asking people if they intend to do something. The mere act of asking people if they intend to vote in an upcoming election, or more powerfully, if they see themselves as the kind of civic-minded citizen who votes, can increase voting by as much

as 25%. You can take this further by asking people to envision *how* and *when* they plan to do it. In one study, 3% of college students got a tetanus shot after listening to a lecture on its importance. If the students got the lecture, but also were given a campus map with the health center circled on it, asked to look at their schedule to identify when they would go, and then check the map for the route they would take, the rate of getting the shot multiplied by over nine-fold to 28% They did not get any new information. They just more clearly mapped out in their own minds the decision and the process to act upon it. In the workplace, this can translate into asking those responsible for innovation, for example, to consider what kind of innovators they want to be, and to map out a plan to make that happen.

There are many other kinds of nudges, from setting up an environment conducive to Vitality to providing better feedback, reducing cognitive load, and better mapping effort to outcomes. In fact, many of the examples described in Chap. 6 on protecting innovation have nudge-like qualities (remember the Hack-a-Thon?). The goal here is not to provide a laundry list of nudge examples, because the list is too long, but instead to encourage the consideration of the environment around Vitality. By embracing imperfect psychology instead of robotic compliance, we can manage change better. But if your appetite for research on human foibles is not yet sated, Chap. 11 will further probe into cognitive biases and heuristics in decision-making.

To conclude this section, remember that nudges are not magical. They will not transform everyone's behavior into that of the most disciplined of dieters, retirement savers, or organizational performers. But they will work on those in the fat part of a bell curve—not the fanatics or the slackers, but the rest of us.

Organizational Support

The sections above on accountability and nudges began to frame the kinds of organizational support that help facilitate organizational change. The overall stage was set in the previous chapter, and by now you know what kind of change is required. Consider the employees most suited to bring about those changes. Are you confident that they—and you—have what is needed to make sustainable change? Are the tools, abilities, resources, and direction available? Keep in mind, the focus is not just on leaders who change their own behavior, as with New Year's resolutions, but on getting others to do things differently, which is even more difficult. So what can leaders do, alongside support staff or other designers of organizational programs, to help promote change to improve Current Performance or build Future Potential?

"Support" is a big topic, and we need to break it down. Overall, there are four aspects on which to focus:

1. **Motivation**. Focusing on those who need to change the most, how inspired or driven to change their behavior are they? Creating motivation involves getting these individuals to buy into overall goals, connecting the vision to the work being done, and making it something they care about. Of course, it is to be expected that different people care about different things. With executives, that might be demonstrating organizational success. With engineers, that might be the opportunity to play with the latest cool technology. Young managers may jump at the chance to demonstrate abilities in front of important people. With anyone, it could be general recognition, a chance to be a part of something important, and, at least to some extent, money.

2. **Prioritization**. It is the responsibility of executives to set priorities that align with the organization's core values and strategy. Individuals have a tendency to set too many priorities. In general, keep the list as short as possible, with a few Current Performance-related priorities and no more than one or two aimed at Future Potential. Do not focus only on what needs the most improvement, but rather prioritize what is most important. Often, prioritization requires balancing one's daily responsibilities with extra improvement efforts.

3. **Guidance**. Even if people are motivated, and know where to focus, taking first steps and sustaining effort to support change is a challenge that requires additional assistance. As with most things outlined in this book, this is more easily available for Current Performance-related issues, because there will be best practices or case studies to examine. However, Future Potential will take you into unchartered waters without the benefit of a map or guide. Nonetheless, you can be as prepared as possible for the journey by doing as much applicable research as possible, and seeking out advice from others who have navigated somewhat similar explorations in order to chart your journey more proactively.

4. **Tracking**. Tracking efforts should launch once change efforts begin. As discussed above, this is putting feedback mechanisms in place to keep track of how well things are progressing. But even if you are not tracking for the purpose of holding individuals or groups accountable, it is still important to track in order to evaluate progress, learn, and make adjustments. Approaches here will definitely also draw from Chap. 7, Evaluating Vitality.

As alluded to above, each of these four aspects of "support" can play differently across changes to improve Current Performance versus those to build Future Potential. Table 9.1 highlights qualities of support for each of these different kinds of pursuits.

Part of the value of a chart like Table 9.1 is that it provides a structure to evaluate where your change is most at risk. At the beginning of this section on organizational support, the question was posed: Are you confident that the pockets of employees involved in creating change have what is needed to succeed? To answer this, first identify whether that change leans more toward Current Performance or Future Potential. Then consider where you might be most at risk: Motivation, Prioritization, Guidance, or Tracking. Clearly all aspects of support will need attention. But if you were to fail, is any one aspect more likely to be to blame? Answers will help inspire how you create the organizational support required to succeed, and then how you weave in nudges or accountabilities to help ensure success.

Tasks That Can Not Be Delegated

As a top leader, you may assign many tasks to your senior management team. However, there are certain items that cannot be passed down. However you define your role in your vital organization, you must be responsible for the following:

- Establishing and communicating strategic context
- Participating in prioritization and goal-setting
- Allocating resources
- Creating commitment and accountability
- Monitoring progress
- Rewarding and recognizing improvement efforts

Table 9.1 Considerations to support change in Current Performance and Future Potential

Aspect of support	Improve Current Performance	Build Future Potential
Motivation	Easier to demonstrate financial benefits	Hard to predict financial benefits
	Can be accomplished in short-term sprints	Requires long-term commitment
	Easier to create specific metrics for rewards	Easier to generate enthusiasm for vision
	May be accomplished within performance-appraisal cycle	Multi-year efforts harder to build into appraisals
Prioritization	Priorities can be framed in terms of existing activities	Priorities will be framed in new language of possibilities
	Research and analyses can help clarify priorities	Priorities clarified as work unfolds
	If things not broken, may be difficult to establish focus	Hard to create "burning platform" if Current Performance is great
Guidance	Expertise may reside within organization	May need to buy, borrow, or invent expertise from scratch
	Possibly executable alongside day-to-day activities	May need large, dedicated blocks of time to execute
	Advice may be more scalable	Advice may be more tailored
	Cross-functional sharing of stories, lessons more possible	Cross-functional leverage may be less relevant
Tracking	Metrics and other evidence more qualitative	Evidence of progress less quantitative
	Milestones tied to dates, results	Milestones tied to learning
	Progress more consistent	Failures will happen

Assessment: Evaluating Your Ability to Make Change Stick

Use the following questions to help gauge your ability not just to live up to your own intentions to change, but to help others to live up to theirs as well:

o The change that needs to happen is well-defined for all involved, including classifying it as Current Performance or Future Potential. (See also Chaps. 3, 4, and 8.)

o The evaluation of the change is well-defined for all involved. (See also Chap. 7.)

o The leaders and individuals most responsible for creating this change have been identified. (Potentially evaluate their strengths according to Chap. 5.)

○ Accountabilities or assignments have been defined and clarified for those required to participate in creating and sustaining the change.

○ There is collective understanding of where the change is most at risk for failure.

Fundamentally, those with change assignments are very well supported regarding:

○ Motivation (inspire or drive change, and provide a rationale, for all who need to act differently)

○ Prioritization (align the change to the overall strategy and focus on a short list)

○ Guidance (help people know how to act and what steps to take)

○ Tracking (evaluate change to hold people accountable as well as to learn)

○ Creative nudges (identified and implemented to help the change process along)

Of the ten items above, the first five cover the set-up, and should be the easiest to endorse. The last five will help the change be sustained over time. Without these last, change will fail. Exactly how you define and provide support (or nudges) will vary dramatically based on what you are trying to accomplish.

To take this and other assessments online, and get an interactive, customized report, visit OV-CVO.com.

CHAPTER 10

Agility and Resiliency

Flexibility Within Boundaries

Agility refers to a company's ability to move quickly, flexibly, and decisively in the face of obstacles, new opportunities, a changing environment or market conditions, or a new strategy. For the vital organization, this includes the ability to react quickly to Future Potential-exploration results, whether they are successful or not. Agile companies learn to "fail fast," moving on quickly from exploration that does not work, but also swiftly turning successful exploration efforts into Current Performance execution.

However, an agile company does more than just act fast. Plenty of companies might move decisively and quickly, and still fail. The trick is to move quickly with underlying systems in place that can support the resulting instabilities caused by changing directions. When explored, agility may seem somewhat paradoxical: Agility is a type of nimbleness or flexibility, yet for a company actually to be agile, it needs a certain amount of structure or rules. While at first this may seem contrary to the idea of agility, it is not. Agility must not be confused with total autonomy. Rather, companies with set policies, structures, or systems in place are more easily able to change directions quickly or make decisions on the fly without negatively affecting the rest of the organization. By ensuring that your organization has high levels of information flow, communication capabilities, and other necessary structures in place, you will enable your employees to move the company forward in a way that corresponds to your underlying vision, principles, or strategy. Think about it: When a company has a set chain of command, clear information flow, and coordination among departments, it is clear who has the decision-making responsibility, and that individual has the information to make and execute changes.[1]

Indeed, this is the model of the US military. You might think at first that military personnel are not agile; they operate within one of the most structured, rules-based organizations that exist. However, think of a commander in the field, who makes immediate decisions within the framework of the military's operating procedures. This is the perfect example of agility with a high level of command and control.

This requires a somewhat nuanced understanding of how—and when—rules enable agility. As described in the example above, rules provide the structure to act quickly and decisively. Too often, however, rules are applied too rigidly, across the board, and without thought or exceptions. Blindly applying rules or following bureaucracy, regardless of the situation, is not optimal, certainly not agile, and can result in unintended consequences or violate the very principles that the organization was looking to uphold by implementing the rules in the first place. This use of rigidly applied rules will prohibit individuals from making commonsense decisions and prevent agility. The purpose of these rules is to allow the organization to make decisions using "standard operating procedures" as a guideline, removing the need for employees to think about most decisions and potentially to make a bad decision. But this also removes the ability to act in a way that benefits the company. Take a customer who calls the help line of a computer maker, upset because her computer has died and she has lost all her family photos. In a non-agile company, a call-center employee may ask about the computer's warranty, and decline to help if the warranty is expired. In an agile company, that same employee may have the freedom to override the warranty-specific rules and help the customer find a solution. You can easily assume which company gets not just the repeat business, but also a "brand ambassador" who tells friends and family members about the wonderful experience with the agile organization.

On the other extreme, companies that operate without any structure may seem aimless; executive decisions may appear random and even inexplicable to those who need to act on them. But it is not the lack of rules or speed at which they turn that make them chaotic; it is the lack of operating principles

---

[1] Atkinson, S.R., Moffat, J., "The Agile Organization: From Informal Networks to Complex Effects and Agility," Office of the Assistant Secretary of Defense (OASD), Command & Control Research Program (CCRP), Washington, DC, 2005.

guiding the decisions being made. Rather than imposing a strict rules-based structure, you want to give employees the freedom to operate within the general framework of the organization. This is especially challenging for large organizations. Bureaucracy is a consequence of scale, and as organizations grow, there may be less sense of community and communication, so more policies and standard practices are put into place. (This is why William Gore, founder of Gore-Tex, imposed a 150-person limit on all of his buildings and factories.) If your company is growing, you need to take care to ensure that rules act as guidelines for effectiveness, and not as barriers to getting things done. Once they stop serving that role, they strangle an organization's performance.

So how does the vital organization implement structure or rules while providing for the flexibility to be agile? It involves applying a principle, rather than a rule. Think again about the help-desk example: A company that tells its employees to adhere strictly to warranties is not agile or flexible. One that tells employees instead to put customer service first, and actually gives them the power to make a decision—whether it is to send a new part free of charge or to stay on the line longer than normal—is being flexible. This is an example of a company that is agile in the moment and on a very local level: A lower-level employee has the ability to make a decision without consulting a superior, which ultimately benefits the company. For a company to be truly agile, it must ensure that all employees have a certain autonomy and flexibility in their daily work. And of course to make that function, employees must be properly prepared so that they can be successful operating in this kind of environment.

Here is a fact about people at work: Employees are not lazy and in general most employees want to do a good job. There is a small portion of employees who do not fit this profile, and unfortunately organizations generally create rules for this subset rather than the majority. They manage for the exception. Isn't it ironic that the average person wants to do a good job, and yet many procedures are created not to deal with the average, but to deal with outliers or exceptions? Isn't this an over-reaction to the occasional abuse? Too often, companies create blanket policies to deal with just a handful of employees who abuse the system, rather than dealing with those individuals specifically. This creates a situation where rules are in place to play defense instead of offense. They are installed to minimize risk instead of maximize value, and are at odds with agility. What can be done in an organization to avoid this pitfall and remain agile?

First, consider a lesson from state-of-the-art manufacturing, which uses mass customization to let a consumer tailor-make a product within a given set of parameters. Instead of sitting on the shelf, the products are instead manufactured as needed to fill a specific order and requirement. If you are reading a paper copy of this book, you are likely reading a copy that was printed to fulfill a company's order, rather than a copy that was printed in a huge run and warehoused until needed, because current printing technology allows for quick production. If you are reading this as an eBook, you produced the book as you downloaded it. That is the ultimate in mass customization flexibility. More generally, the use of technology allows the orders to be completed in a fashion and at a speed similar to or better than traditionally mass-produced items. The days of Ford's "you can have it in any color you want as long as that color is black" are rapidly disappearing. Consider the Converse sneaker company, which has found a lot of success letting customers design their own shoes, from the print on the canvas down to the color of the eyelets. This concept of mass customization can be successfully applied to other organizational policies and practices, not just to manufacturing. Many companies stop short of mass customization, and offer customers instead the ability to configure products or services within an existing framework of options. However, the most agile—and indeed, the most successful—companies move beyond configuration and actually customize products or services for their customers and have figured out, like Converse, how to do so at scale.

Second, as discussed earlier in this book, organizations need to examine the behaviors they are encouraging and rewarding, whether intentionally or not. Organizations get the behavior that they actually recognize and reinforce, not necessarily that which they espouse. Consider supervisors who are given recognition rewards to distribute to their employees, yet who are themselves rewarded for coming in under budget. How do you come in under budget? One way is to not give out recognition rewards! It is often a very healthy exercise for an organization to review what they are actually rewarding, as opposed to what they think they are rewarding.

Third, inject new energy into organizations to adapt to changing environments, market realities, or new technologies. Current Performance takes energy: You need a certain amount to maintain the work you do on a daily basis. The pursuit of Future Potential is to ensure your business remains relevant after your Current Performance starts to get stale. At the point in the cycle when you transition from Future Potential to Current Performance, you need to inject a greater deal of energy—time, resources, and effort—in order to break the existing paradigm and re-invent. Staying agile allows you to be alert and poised to implement change quickly when needed. This means you must carefully consider all processes and procedures to make sure they support agility. This could be achieved simply, such as with a willingness to run non-routine situations up the line for approval or review by higher levels—or, even better, to drive down the decision-making process so that the non-routine can be handled locally. The key is examining your current work systems and making improvements that help your organization become more agile.

Fourth, employees are taught to think only inside the box using standard solutions to tackle any problems because companies tend to establish rules to prevent unique or non-traditional approaches. They learn to deal with the average situation by behaving in a more average fashion. This is clearly not what you want from an employee. Agility means encouraging diversity in thinking and approach—in fact welcoming even negative or mediocre feedback—because this is how individuals and organizations learn and grow developmentally. This way, when the situation is no longer average or typical, employees—and therefore the organization—can adapt. This is the "embrace of variance," which means accepting information-rich feedback—average responses usually have more information in them than either very positive or very negative responses—that may be purposely less than universally favorable, so that you can learn where pockets of exceptionally good and poor performance exist within the organization. This method will also mean that, when faced with novel situations, the solution and ability to deal with it may already exist inside the organization. If you are pursuing employee or customer feedback, do not structure your survey or questions in a way that will just achieve some feel-good, highly uniform, favorable results, because that will not teach you anything. Instead, figure out the tough questions to ask that truly allow your company to evolve. Mid-range scores, which contain more variance and hence more information, may be more painful to see, but mean that there are likely parts of the organization that are operating better than other parts, which can be studied to see how they achieved their results. This enables you to become a self-learning organization and is potentially much more powerful than any external benchmarks.

None of this is easy. In a recent study done by the management consulting firm McKinsey & Company, only 12% of companies surveyed were considered agile.[2] The rest either moved too slowly, or moved fast but without the stability in place to make them agile. According to the report, agility has a huge impact on an organization's overall health and success.

Oftentimes, agile organizations stem from leaders who are considered "Learning Agile."[3] These are individuals who not only accept challenges, but also pause to reflect on success and failure, welcome feedback from diverse sources, and continuously question their own behaviors and assumptions. People who are Learning Agile tend to be trailblazers, willingly putting themselves in situations where success is far from guaranteed in order to learn new skill sets. The greatest learning opportunities come from new challenges and experiences, but in order to actually learn from them, an individual must remain engaged and able to adapt quickly. Learning Agile individuals do this more quickly, enabling them to pick up more skills and handle stress more easily than others.

Entropy and Agility

Entropy is the eventual decline from order to chaos. Applied to the business realm, it means that even the best-working systems, left unattended, will eventually become useless, and that existing energies will falter. Every aspect of business—as with life in general—has to cope with entropy. In fact, there are so many ways to have disorder—and only one way or a small number of ways to have perfect order—that you will generally always have to cope with some level of disorder. That is completely normal and to be expected. This is where being agile is especially important: It enables you to react and adapt to minimize the disruptive forces affecting your business. Here is an example: Most companies hire employees to fill a specific position which has been laboriously defined in terms of knowledge, skills, and abilities (KSA). But strict adherence to the requisite KSA is rarely possible and this ideal can make it difficult to staff a position, because you will forever be searching for that perfect candidate. Rather, find dynamic individuals who fit the culture

[2] Bazigos, M., De Smet, A., and Gagnon, C., "Why Agility Pays," *McKinsey Quarterly*, October 2015.
[3] Mitchinson, A. and Morris, R., "Learning about Learning Agility," Center for Creative Leadership.

of the organization, who have the basic skill sets, and in general can benefit the organization, and then build the position around them by playing to their strengths and compensating for their weaknesses. No two project managers will be alike, for example. One might be better at presentations, while the other excels at data management. This does not mean one is better than the other, but rather that they can both benefit your company in different ways.

For instance, say you are a department manager and able to design the "perfect" organization, with each person having just the right skill sets in place for optimal performance. In this world, your work is getting done like a choreographed ballet: It is on time, on budget, and has high levels of customer satisfaction. But then a new person—an element of randomness—gets placed within your department with the task of examining existing methods, processes, and work in order to improve them. This person is highly creative and energetic, but just can't seem to operate according to department norms, sowing disorder in his or her path. What do you do? One possibility is to eliminate that person from the department and go back to the "normal" way of doing things. That is certainly the easier path, which requires less energy expenditure. But you need to ask yourself what you would be losing: What fresh ideas or operational improvements will not get thought up and tested if you eliminate this person? In order to effectively utilize this employee's capabilities, you must be willing to make the necessary adjustments to keep your ballet well-choreographed, while challenging existing procedures in order to become more efficient in the long term. When you evaluate potential improvements, adopting those that work and rejecting those that don't, you are being agile. This is an especially important consideration for senior management. Even the most successful CEOs have their weaknesses, and it is very common for organizations to build compensating mechanisms to deal with those shortcomings.

To reduce chaos and increase agility, organizations need to expend energy to build order into the system. Systems get an "energy" input that creates order, only to begin a run down toward entropy, until more energy is invested into the system from the outside. As discussed, order must mean not just rules, but rather systems that let employees operate in a fashion that achieves the organization's goals. Order enables people who are aligned and knowledgeable about what needs to get done to have the freedom to do it. Order allows for better, more consistent performance, and the ability to inject energy when needed.

The Aging Organization

Why do we age? The easy answer is that time passes and we grow older, and with age comes a deterioration of physical and mental abilities. Organizations also feel the effect of time, but whereas the elderly may face ageism or other discrimination, many older organizations are considered successful, enduring, trustworthy, and reliable—at least until something drastic happens that changes the industry. Then, if the older organization struggles to adapt, its age shifts to the negative connotation of being obsolete.

What makes an organization resist the negative effects of aging? To answer this question, it's important to look at some of the longest-lasting companies, such as the oldest company in the world, a Japanese-based construction company that was founded in 578 AD and liquidated in 2007. Four of the next ten oldest companies are either breweries or wineries, two are hotels, one is a restaurant, one produces salt, one is a foundry making bells, and one makes religious artifacts. What do these oldest-of-the-old companies have in common? Many are still run by the founding families and some boast of being run by the 40th-plus generation. These resilient companies have managed to survive through wars, recessions, depressions, catastrophes, succession issues, changing technology, markets, and managements.

Organizations clearly go through life-cycles or aging, from start-up to middle age, to maturity, and finally to old age. And while some are able to survive for the long term, others pass through these "life stages" rather quickly. The life stages that an organization experiences might not be as closely tied to the passage of time as human aging, but instead to organizational behaviors that can occur at any time after the organization's founding. One has to wonder if older organizations—those exhibiting signs of later life stages—should be revitalized or allowed to pass away, and whether any insight can be gained by comparing what happens to individuals as they age versus what happens to organizations as they age into more advanced life stages.

A story in the *New York Times* describes what may be clues to a lucid human old age, typically enjoyed by only one out of 200 of us.[4] "These are the most successful agers on earth, and they are only just beginning to teach us what's important, in their genes, in their routines, in their lives," said Dr. Claudia Kawas a neurologist at University of California at Irvine. "We think, for example, that it is very important to use your brain, to keep challenging your mind, but all mental activity may not be equal. We're seeing some evidence that a social component may be crucial."

[4] Carey, B., "At the Bridge Table, Clues to a Lucid Old Age," *New York Times*, May 22, 2009.

It is speculated that aging in humans is caused by an accumulation of both biological and sociological factors. Among the biological factors are: wear and tear, meaning that the body simply wears out from constant use just as a machine would; autoimmune issues, such as the tendency of the body to reject its own tissues over time; free-radical buildup, which is the notion that certain chemical compounds accumulate over time causing damage and aging; programmed cellular deterioration, or the notion that every organism is programmed to die after a certain number of years, possibly because it adds to reproductive and survival fitness at the species level; somatic mutations, or an accumulation of mutations eventually resulting in functional failure and death; and homeostatic imbalance or the inability of the body to maintain stable levels of various chemical elements over the long term.

In addition to biological failings, there are social patterns that tend to impact an individual's rate of aging both positively and negatively. These include disengagement, the gradual withdrawal of the individual from society; the loss of role, self-identity, and self-esteem associated with retirement; children moving away; or other major life changes. A decrease in activity is often followed by increased deterioration. Continuity can compensate with the substitution of new roles for lost ones, which slows the aging process (e.g., volunteering or finding a second career).

Let us speculate a bit on how the theories used to describe human aging might be used to describe organizational aging.

Wear and tear: The equivalent notion for organizations would be to just keep doing what the organization has done before and been successful at, without re-examining assumptions or approaches to the business. Over time, the tried and true might just wear out as it becomes more and more obsolete. This is focus on Current Performance to the exclusion of building Future Potential.

Autoimmune issues: There is a standard joke that the definition of a consultant is someone who comes from more than 50 miles away. This pokes fun at the fact that too many organizations reject the advice given by internal staff because they are too familiar. A heavy dependence on external consultants while disregarding internal staff and rejecting their ideas could be a contributing factor to organizational aging. Free-radical buildup: This would be the notion that organizations continue to put band-aids on their problems rather than fixing the legacy issues and systems that are the root cause. Over time, the buildup of band-aids can cause the entire system to collapse and certainly opens the door to competitors not encumbered with the legacy systems. This is a lack of the agility characteristic of recognizing when something is failing and then putting it aside.

Programmed cellular theory: This is one of the more interesting notions. We die because it is in the best interests of the species that we die so that more fit offspring with adaptations potentially better suited to the current environment can take our place. If we were to live forever there would be slower reproduction and evolutionary changes, making the species more vulnerable to extinction should the environment change. If this is correct, you could draw the conclusion that organizations that have "run their course" should be allowed to fold, so that more evolutionarily fit versions can arise to take their place. This would occur through lack of building Future Potential.

Somatic mutations: Organizations that continually mutate by trying new things in an effort to always grow will eventually build up enough unsuccessful components that organizational death will occur. (To read more about this, see Jim Collins' "undisciplined pursuit of more."[5])

Homeostatic theory: This is the inability of the organization to maintain stable levels of various needed elements over the long term, such as innovation, risk-taking, entrepreneurship, meritocracy, integrity, and the like. This type of aging comes about when the necessary balance between Current Performance and Future Potential is missing.

The key to a long life as an organization? Constant renewal. Doing what you do well, but reinventing yourself to compensate for the changing environment and needs of your customers.

Resiliency

Organizational resiliency is the capacity of a company to anticipate, respond, and acclimate to both incremental and sudden changes. Organizations that are resilient gracefully adapt to stressors in the environment. Resilient organizations, as previously discussed, have learned to "fail fast" and to find value in their failures. On the individual level, a resilient person is someone who overcomes obstacles or defeat and tries again, and who welcomes feedback as a learning experience. For corporations, this may mean experiencing many innovation failures, but learning from them and trying again. This also refers to setting up systems that can quickly adapt to changing circumstances. Resiliency can change over time. The good news is that it can be learned and improved at the organizational, systemic, and individual levels. But it will decline in the organization if it is not actively supported and championed.

[5] Collins, J., "How the Mighty Fall," *Businessweek*, May 2009.

Any organization can be resilient, whether it is a family-run farm, Etsy shop owner, large private-sector corporation, or governmental or educational institution. There are three main ways you can help your organization be resilient:

Mitigate External Environmental Factors

External environmental factors are things outside of your organization that may also be out of your control, such as weather-related disasters, foreign-government decisions, disruptive competitors entering your market, economic turmoil, and so on. To cope with these, companies must be vigilant about monitoring or collecting information about the current status of the risks that might affect their business. Be proactive and anticipate the challenges you may be facing, instead of waiting for them to impact the business before mitigating them. When these risks materialize and negatively impact your business, it is important to compartmentalize them to the specific affected area, so that one or two troublesome problems do not have a downward-spiraling effect on the entire business.

Invest in Internal Organizational Capabilities

You can beef up your company's resiliency by investing in your people, products, and processes in order to make the company stronger as a whole. Challenges are more easily handled when people, products, and processes are strong. Make sure your vision, values, and operating style are shared throughout the organization. They provide an organizational-standards roadmap for people, so that they are better equipped to deal with challenges they face. Turn risks into opportunities by developing a culture of innovation and by creating organizational capabilities, such as rewarding innovative ideas and performance, creating bench strength, or tapping into the diversity of talent and developing it. Finally, it is important to enhance the tools within your company in order to increase organizational effectiveness (e.g., cost control, state-of-the-art business processes, or contingency planning), and to ensure that your employees have the best available tools or products and processes to accomplish their work.

Recognition of Organizational Achievement

This pertains to celebrating or rewarding both organizational and personal accomplishments, such as successful completion of goals. Recognize a job well done, an obstacle overcome, a significant milestone being accomplished, or the obtaining of significant new knowledge, skills, and abilities. Companies achieve this by installing robust reward and recognition systems. Providing these recognitions of achievement to people is like putting money in the bank that you can withdraw as needed later.

Resilient Leaders

While resiliency, as an academically defined term, has been most widely studied with children who grow up in poverty, almost every successful entrepreneur or business leader exhibits at least some of the characteristics associated with resiliency, such as seeing obstacles as opportunities, or not being afraid to give up and move on when something is not working. Renowned child-psychology professor and resiliency expert Ann Masten wrote, "The greatest surprise of resilience research is the ordinariness of the phenomenon."[4] People in general are resilient and can bounce back from and overcome challenges if given the support and opportunity to do so. Dealing with and recovering quickly from challenges is critical to the long-term success of all our endeavors. How does a child raised in poverty in the Bronx rise to become a Supreme Court judge, or another born in Harlem, raised in the South Bronx by Jamaican immigrant parents, serve as Chairman of the Joints Chiefs of Staff as well as Secretary of State, or a child raised by a teen mom in an unstable environment rise to become president of the United States? These were not children of privilege; these were children of resilience.

In business, as in life, there will always be things that go wrong: Data systems will be breached, quality control issues will arise, disruptive forces will enter your market, or critical employees will retire or become ill. It is unrealistic to think that an organization can exist in a bubble, cut off from any effects brought about by an ever-changing, increasingly complex, and globalizing environment.

[4] Masten, A.S., "Ordinary Magic: Resilience Processes in Development," *American Psychologist*, vol. 56, Number 3, 227–238, March 2001.

Today's environment—technologically, socially, and globally—is more volatile than ever, and the pace of change shows no sign of slowing down. Being continuously hit by new and unpredictable challenges will, ironically, become more and more routine. Responding effectively to these non-normal challenges is now more important than ever. Organizations need to be equipped to face them with plans that build in resiliency. Coping with current challenges in a sustainable fashion and with responses that do not limit future options or choices is critical to resiliency in responding to tomorrow's challenges.

In order to build resiliency, company leaders must try to keep their options open and flexible. When making decisions, these leaders should choose the path that provides flexibility, even if it does not otherwise seem like the best path to take. For example, a company can choose to source product materials from a variety of vendors, as opposed to just one, in case one of the vendors has problems completely unrelated to—and uncontrolled by—the company. It may not be as cost-effective initially as using just one vendor, but could provide options should a problem arise. Of course, you can never eliminate all potential threats to your organization, but you can put systems and options into place to give you more flexibility to deal with challenges.

Ultimately, the most successful organizations are the ones that build systems and structures that promote both agility and resiliency. These are complementary tools to use in your quest for Vitality, and having one helps you have the other. As the current environment changes, agility allows your organization to make the necessary changes, while being resilient enables it to weather the bumps, allowing order to be restored for the time being. Agility and resiliency help companies navigate the waters of "failing fast" on their Future Potential explorations. It is up to Vitality-oriented leaders to set up the culture and systems that make a company agile and resilient, recognizing that natural entropy or other disruptive forces can help the company move forward.

Assessment: Evaluating Your Agility and Resiliency

Do you have the right kinds of adaptability to adjust to unforeseen changes in the environment, as well as to quickly learn from and adjust as you explore Future Potential? To help you break this down in your evaluation, consider the statements below, five covering agility and five covering resilience, and whether they reflect the reality of your organization (adapted from Fig. 7.1):

Agility

○ We actively and widely scan for new information about what is going on.
○ We quickly and clearly make sense of ambiguous or uncertain situations.
○ We are open to change.
○ We take advantage of opportunities quickly.
○ We quickly deploy or re-deploy resources to support execution.

Resiliency

○ We have clearly defined and widely held values and beliefs.
○ We have a strong sense of identity and purpose that can survive anything.
○ We have a strong support network of external alliances or partnerships.
○ We are expanding our external alliances and partnerships.
○ We have "deep pockets"—access to capital and resources to weather anything.

If you can check four or five within each topic area, you do well with each of these topics. If you only checked three, you may have some sound building blocks, but have some work to do. If you can only check one or two within each area, you have some serious rigidity to overcome.

To take this and other assessments online, and get an interactive, customized report, visit OV-CVO.com.

CHAPTER 11

Decision-Making

Decision-Making Despite Environmental and Human Conditions

Pick up the business section of a major newspaper any day of the week, and you will find myriad examples of organizations making both minor and major decisions that have the potential to have a huge impact on their business, either positively or negatively. Take movie-studio executives charged with deciding which projects to greenlight. Some, such as sequels to a popular movie, are easy decisions. Others, such as taking a chance on a new genre or topic, may be more risky, and could either flop or become blockbuster successes. Thousands of decisions are made—such as who will direct or star in the movie, how much to invest in its making, and when it will be released—that all contribute to its ultimate success for failure. How did management in each of those cases make decisions regarding which movies to make, how much to spend on them, and when to release them? What affected their decision to stick to the tried-and-true versus exploring new genres?

As previously discussed, the ability to optimize Vitality within an organization is affected by clearly articulating a vision and strategy, by the structure the organization assumes, as well as by the capabilities of those chosen to inhabit the organization (openness to new ideas vs. sticking with the tried-and-true). But chief among the factors affecting the ability to operate as a vital organization are the decision-making abilities of the top leaders. No one is immune from the biases surrounding human cognitive processes, but being aware of them—and of how they affect one's decisions—is a huge step toward improving your abilities in this area.

Heuristics or Rules-of-Thumb

Executives at a large food manufacturing company were concerned. They looked at the employees who worked on their production lines, most of whom were women, and wondered how working at such a monotonous, boring job impacted their work. They brought in a company to conduct an employee survey. The results shocked them: Not only did the women enjoy their work, which they could do while socializing and forget about when they walked out the door at the end of the shift, but these women also wondered how the executives could possibly stand the stressful, all-consuming nature of their work. One moral of this story is that people have trouble seeing the world from other perspectives. As we will discuss in the next chapter, most humans are driven by similar underlying desires. However, the way these desires are fulfilled will be different depending on the individual. You might relate to one side more than the other, but the point is that everyone sees the world from their own, unique perspective. What may seem like boring work to one person is fascinating, or at least rewarding, to another.

How do we make these kinds of judgments? Sigmund Freud said, "When you meet a human being, the first distinction you make is whether the person is male or female, and you are accustomed to making that distinction with unhesitating certainty." You make that distinction with unhesitating certainty because of heuristics or rules-of-thumb you have regarding body shapes, facial characteristics, et cetera, that are classified as female or male. Heuristics speed up the decision-making process by providing mental short-cuts that enable quicker judgments. People tend to build mental models to cope with the vast amount of information coming our way daily. The ability to develop these models is hardwired into our brains; the ability developed with us as we developed, even as we evolved as a species, because it provided a survival advantage. The specific models we develop over time arise from experience, training, upbringing, or exposure to various sources of information. These models speed decision-making by reducing information-processing time within the brain. Everyone has built useful and accurate models. But most have also built models based on flawed assumptions or poor information, and some have also built models based on bias, bigotry, or worse. These mental models are seductive, for they simplify the world in which we live, boiling down complexities to basic rules.

By definition, heuristics may not lead to perfect decisions, but they are instrumental in navigating the world without requiring too much thought or concentration about simple matters. That person on the train, sitting with her eyes closed and earbuds in? Clearly a good seatmate if you are hoping to get work done on your commute. That is a heuristic helping you make a snap judgment.

However, heuristics can lead you to the wrong decision if you are not careful, because of the flawed assumptions or biases involved. Consider hospital janitors, who spend their days dealing with hospital waste. Sounds like a horrible job, right? Heuristics lead most people to assume that. However, studies show that hospital custodians report some of the highest rates of job satisfaction because they find meaning in their work, helping people and their families during difficult times. This is similarly true for Disney "cast members" who work as groundskeepers at the parks. They receive a two-week training course prior to starting work that empowers them to help families who may be lost, or to replace a child's dropped ice cream. The nature of their work makes them feel integral to visitors' experiences at Disney, becoming brand ambassadors, and as a result, greatly increases their job satisfaction.

So, how do you avoid falling into these common decision-making traps? Renowned psychologists Daniel Kahneman and Amos Tversky[1] extensively researched common foibles that humans are prone to and which can be especially important in organizational decision-making. To make better decisions, it is important to be aware of the following:

- **Optimism and Loss Aversion:** When considering investments in either Current Performance or Future Potential, people tend to be optimistic about the expected benefits and discount the potential for loss. For example, when investing in new product or service developments, many people will underestimate costs while overestimating value. This can complicate exploration or innovation efforts, many of which fail. Before you make a major decision, use all available evidence and metrics—as described in Chap. 7—to get the most likely prediction of costs or return on investments so that you are using the most reliably accurate figure.

---

[1] Kahneman, D., Tversky, A. *Judgment under Uncertainty: Heuristics and Bias*, (Cambridge University Press, 1974).

- **Sunk costs:** This is the tendency to continue pursuing an idea or project because a great deal of time or money has already been invested: The more "sunk" into a project, the greater the tendency to continue to invest in an effort to salvage what has already been invested. Sunk costs can also be described by the idiom "throwing good money after bad." This is a direct threat to the notion of Vitality. It is why so many organizations sway more heavily to the Current Performance side of their business, since that is where most of the resources have been invested. It also interferes with the notion of failing fast, or abandoning projects as soon as you realize they are not working out, which is critical for companies as they explore Future Potential. Once committed and invested in a path, humans find it increasingly difficult to veer from that path as the path is traveled.

- **Availability:** When decision-makers are sitting around a table debating which course of action to take, such as where to focus on Current Performance or where to invest in the future, there is a tendency to give more value to the options discussed during the session. In other words, if a possibility easily springs to mind, most people will consider it more relevant than other options. Closely related is Kahnman's concept of "What you see is all there is," or "WYSIATI," which means that people only take into account the options that are in front of them at the time. So when making a decision, individuals will likely consider the choices that are presented and not look for alternate options, because people tend to assume that the best path or choice is among those that have been discussed. Rarely do people consider going back to the drawing board to bring forth new and different options. This type of decision-making also favors Current Performance, and is a real threat to building Future Potential.

- **Anchoring:** This is when someone offers a figure as a starting point. Other people will be influenced by that number, and use it as a reference point. For example, if a CEO predicts that the company will make a certain amount of money from an investment, all other guesses will revolve around that number. It is better for all bets to be placed privately in order to find the most accurate prediction. Just as it is important to know what questions to ask, knowing which numbers are important to consider, while avoiding irrelevant numbers, is one important way to improve decision-making.

- **Conjunction fallacy:** This is when more detailed explanations are given greater weight than simple ones. Say you are the CEO of a company looking to build a new plant. One employee comes and gives you the basic cost of building the site in Chicago, while another, tasked with looking at California, gives you not just the basic cost of building, but includes the high quality of schools, access to major roadways, and other details. The more detailed option will feel like a better choice, but that is not necessarily the case. When making a decision, make sure you are either comparing options with the same amount of background information, or be aware that you may be more likely to favor the option with more details for the wrong reasons.

- **Framing:** This is when a question, or a decision choice, is framed in a way that influences your decision. (Most companies do this when they structure sales in a certain way so as to attract more buyers.) Here's an example: You are more likely to invest in Future Potential work if it is presented as having a 90% chance of being successful than you would if it was presented to you as having a 10% chance of failure. Framing can push you in a certain direction, depending on how the decision is worded. If you are being presented with a choice by employees who have a stake in your decision, it is important to consider carefully how they are framing the question.

So how do you ensure that none of the heuristics described negatively affect your judgment? In part by surrounding yourself with a diversity of opinions and senior leadership-team members who are not afraid to question or contradict their boss. Make sure you are considering all the various possibilities, outcomes, and perspectives before making a decision. Try and be aware of when you are making assumptions, and take care to learn whether they are true before acting on them. Solicit independently derived options that are made individually, as opposed to in a group setting.

Understanding Your Judgment

People have a tendency to think that their judgments are better than they are. While most individuals like to believe that they act in a rational manner, most judgments and decisions are affected by underlying biases and heuristics. For example, it has been documented that 95% of Americans are certain that they are above-average drivers. In a leadership study, 25% of those participating were confident that they were in the top 1% in leadership ability. Another study showed that 40% of street-gang members were certain that one day they would be the leader of the gang. Clearly, people have higher optimism about their abilities and judgments than is mathematically possible.

This is due to the self-confidence bias, in which people are very confident of their abilities and judgments. Often, individuals will overestimate their actual performance, or think more highly about their performance relative to others. This is dangerous, because leaders often believe that they have the expertise to make decisions when they do not, and they trust their decisions more than they should. While this affects most individuals, some leaders and organizations also display hubris or arrogance when it comes to their decisions. Jim Collins, author of *How the Mighty Fall,* explains that success can lead to arrogance, and cause leaders to stop looking at the underlying reasons for their success and come to expect it naturally. They can make marginal decisions, assuming that their previous successes will carry them through, or that they know best regardless of objective evidence or what others suggest. These people discount the role of luck or chance, and also stop continuously striving for improvement. Better leaders, while certainly equipped with a certain amount of self-confidence and pride, realize that success is not an entitlement, but rather something always to work toward. Leaders who welcome diverse or even contrary opinions, as well as feedback, are taking a large step toward overcoming this bias.

Here's another example that directly impacts organizational staffing: Interviewers are certain that they can add predictive value, beyond objective measures, in terms of how people will perform on the job. However, there is significant evidence, dating back to the 1940s, that proves this is simply not the case, and in fact interviewers can muddy the waters, yielding poorer hiring decisions than objective measures alone.[2] These beliefs persist, even though they cannot possibly be true, and pervade all aspects of your life beyond business. Common folk wisdom often contradicts itself and is applied to situations as it conveniently fits in order to "prove" a point. Consider the proverbs "absence makes the heart grow fonder" and "out of sight, out of mind." People will choose one of these contradictory statements that seems to fit the situation best and say, "See, there is a rule, a precedent for that." We fool ourselves about our decision-making prowess every single day.

Common sense is based on your belief system, and driven by assumptions—sometimes based on heuristics—that are not based on factual evidence and therefore may be fundamentally incorrect. The ancient Greeks made sense of lightning by attributing it to the behavior of Zeus, helping to make sense of a world that previously made no sense to them. Of course, we know today that this was a myth, and tend to think of it as some cute bedtime parable told to children as we try to calm their fears of the flashes and sounds of a storm, but to the Greeks it was real. Now, you may think this ancient example does not apply to the modern world, but there are still many things we assume that may be incorrect. For years, many scientists believed that Earth was likely the only planet with life because the confluence of conditions found on our planet was assumed to be rare and that fragile life needed Goldilocks conditions that were just so. Now, however, scientists believe that the conditions that allow life to flourish here are not unique to our planet, solar system, or galaxy, and that it is just a matter of time until we find life elsewhere. The questions you face may be more of the earthly realm, but just as important to the life of your organization. Ask yourself what assumptions are driving your decisions, and try to understand the principles behind performance and the laws governing it, and not simply base your decision-making on commonsense wisdom.

When gathering evidence to make a decision, the way you ask a question matters greatly, just as the way a question posed to you will affect your answer. When you set up a question in a certain way, you are likely to get the answer you want, or the one you think you already know. Here is a story

[2] Sarbin, (1943); Two methods for predicting success of University of Minnesota undergrads in 1939; Meyer, H., (1956), "An Evaluation of a Supervisory Selection Program," *Personnel Psychology*, Vol. 9, (4); Highhouse, S., (2008), "Stubborn Reliance on Intuition and Subjectivity in Employee Selection," *Industrial Organizational Psychology*, Vol. 1, (3).

that illustrates that point. Say you had 100 people spaced at regular intervals wrapped around the equator of the earth and your goal is to determine the shape of the Earth. Is it flat or round? Perhaps oblong? You consider which questions you should be asking and you settle upon this: "In which direction does the sun rise, travel, and set?" This is a good set of questions that will give you some insight into the conditions that your observers are experiencing in their respective locations. Every one of your observers would give you a similar answer. To those standing on the equator, the sun is seen as rising in the east, travelling across the sky and then setting in the west. From that answer one might conclude or at least find no contradictory evidence to the commonly held notion, at one point in time, that the Earth was indeed flat. And this answer would match the evidence you can see with your very own eyes, which makes a persuasive, compelling argument. But what is lost in all of this is that the wrong question is being asked. If you had the ability for simultaneous communication and asked those same equatorially based 100 people, "Right now, at this moment in time, where is the sun?" their answers would lead to quite a different conclusion regarding the shape of the Earth, and you would have to have enough confidence in your method, and ability to interpret the responses, to contradict the evidence you see with your own eyes.

So how do you know the right questions to ask? Sometimes, it is a matter of simply asking multiple questions from a variety of perspectives. Consider the question as it affects not just short-term Current Performance, but also the Future Potential of your business. Then, consider all the stakeholders, and how they would pose the questions. Encourage others in your organization to create some questions as well. Imagine a client asks your business for some work. Your first inclination might be to ask your top leadership team, "How can we get this done for them quickly?" And the answer may be to turn to a specific department—perhaps your IT department—to do the work for the client. However, you could ask other questions as well, such as, "Is there a way we can build a platform that enables this client, and maybe others, to procure this type of work more regularly?" Instead of just answering the initial question from a Current Performance perspective, you are looking at it from various angles to see how it might help your Future Potential explorations.

Attractiveness of Judgment

What draws people in both organizations and in everyday life to erroneous judgments based on gut intuition, commonly held heuristics, or information-processing tendencies due to the fundamental wiring of our brains, rather than ones based on scientific evidence? Scott Highhouse, a psychologist at Bowling Green University and author of *Judgement and Decision Making at Work* explains with a three-part answer: First, people value the flexibility that judgment-based decisions provide, as they are open to interpretation and nuance, while data-driven approaches tend to be inflexible and formulaic. Next, people who are making the judgment operate on gut instinct, and often lack insight into how they derived their prediction. In other words, they feel that they just "know" the right judgment, but in reality they are easily seduced by irrelevant information that affects their judgments. Lastly, people do not tolerate error (they tend to rationalize things if their judgments prove wrong), while the scientific method, based on probability, accepts error as inevitable. It is part of the measurement process and part of scientific investigations.

Improve Your Decision-Making Abilities

The first step in making better decisions is understanding when cognitive biases and heuristics are more likely to kick in or lead you astray. The conditions are very similar to those well-suited to nudging, as discussed in Chap. 9—unfamiliarity, low feedback, high cognitive load. Add to that high pressure or stress to make the decision, or which otherwise drive a "need for closure," and you have a recipe for bias. Exactly what biases or mental shortcuts will be used are unclear, but these are the conditions where we are more likely to fall back on our old habits, patterns, paradigms, and stereotypes. When those are fit poorly with reality, we make bad decisions. As you might expect, this is much more likely to be true with Future Potential decisions, where not just a single individual but no one within the organization is familiar with the new territory. Some people are better at resisting biases and heuristics: These are the same Vitality-oriented leaders described in Chap. 5.

However, there are concrete steps you can take to improve your decision-making abilities. Start with devoting your full attention to complex tasks. Way too many people think they can successfully multi-task their way through their day, but they are wrong. In fact, even the word "multi-task" is a misnomer: What you are really doing is task-switching, and this can greatly reduce your productivity, while also negatively affecting your decision-making abilities. Studies show that you can lose up to 40% productivity when you move back and forth between tasks, such as writing a report and checking e-mail, and that, the more complex or unfamiliar the tasks, the more productivity that is lost.[3] Yet too many people think they can successfully navigate between tasks or thoughts, leading to distraction, errors in action, behaviors, decisions, and judgment. Put down your phone, close the lid on your laptop, stop e-mailing, and listen! Be fully present.

Upon hearing this advice in class, one MBA student turned off his cell phone and computer screen while talking to his employee during a work-planning meeting so he wouldn't be tempted by e-mail. He focused and paid attention to what the employee was saying, making the employee the center of his attention. They made decisions about where and what to work on together. In class the following week, the student reported that the results were remarkable. The employee's behavior began to improve immediately. He stated that the employee who traditionally left at 5:00 p.m. on the dot started to stay later and put in extra effort. If his boss was clearly focused on his work, then his work must be very important, and he was going to treat it that way. Remember that, in general, people want to do a good job and will give it their all if you create the right conditions. Giving the employee his attention fueled that employee's performance and created a stronger connection between the boss and subordinate. Operating within the Vitality framework is complex, with many decisions needing to be made regarding the allocation of resources and what to do when. Focused attention helps you deal with the complexities inherent in that. Stop multi-tasking. Learn how to focus. Cultivate your ability to laser in on the conversation or the decision at hand. Since Current Performance execution and Future Potential exploration have such different needs, try attending to them separately, setting aside time to review priorities related to each. Modeling these behaviors will affect the behaviors of your employees, especially where technology is concerned.

Second, learn how to see things from another's perspective, and learn how to consider the decision as if the outcome of the decision, its impact, were to have an unknown effect on you personally. In other words, you could be on the positive or negative end of a decision, and whether it would affect you in a positive or negative manner was completely unknown and unknowable

---

[3] Rubinstein, J., Evans, J., and Meyer, D., 2001.

to you. The "Veil of Ignorance," a thought experiment by the philosopher John Rawls, is often used in ethics or morality classes to teach this practice. Students are urged to ignore how a specific decision might affect them, including whether or not the decision will be to their advantage. Now, what is the right decision? Consider PepsiCo, which launched a serious sustainability effort under the leadership of Indra Nooyi, who was raised in a country where there are increasing concerns about fresh-water scarcity. Would a Western-born leader have made the same decisions, or—as these sustainability efforts have proved very profitable—seen the same opportunities?

You can never fully walk in someone else's shoes. However, you can try to explore their perspectives. As you balance the competing needs of Current Performance and Future Potential, making decisions about resources and other issues, consider how your decisions directly impact those charged with maintaining Current Performance versus those building Future Potential. This does not mean that you will always make a universally agreed-upon decision, especially as you move resources from one part of the business to another. Rather, it will help you better understand how your decisions impact everyone within your organization, and will likely help you communicate your decisions in a way that most employees can accept.

Sometimes a decision can be shown to be mathematically fair, and yet will be perceived as unfair. Imagine that a small child knocks on your door, selling lottery tickets for a well-known local charity. There will be only 10 tickets sold for $100 apiece, and the winner will receive a new car. There is one ticket left, with the nine others purchased by nine separate individuals, so each person has an equal one in ten chance to win. Many would jump at the opportunity to support the charity and spend $100 on a 10% chance for a new car. Now, imagine that instead of the nine other tickets being bought by and spread over nine other individuals, the child informs you that her dad already bought the other nine tickets and you could buy the last one. Does that feel the same to you? You still have a 10% chance at the new car, but her dad has a 90% chance. Doesn't seem quite right or fair does it? And yet, mathematically it is an absolutely identical situation. You had a 10% chance of winning the car under the first scenario and a 10% chance of winning the car under the second. The only thing that has changed is whether you have an equal chance of winning as the other participants. As discussed earlier, this "framing" is an example of process fairness, or lack thereof, and illustrates how important positioning a decision or choice is in determining how people will react to it. Think about the taxes you pay to the government. While many complain of the level of taxation, what really gets people upset is if a person or a class of people is perceived as receiving unfair treatment, getting a benefit, or a tax loophole or rate that is not universally available. The perceived lack of fairness is a major reason why some people, who otherwise would never break a law, cheat on their taxes: They are simply trying to gain back some of the fairness that they feel has been lost.

Third, examine whether your decision will violate "norms of behavior." Not that there is anything wrong with pushing the envelope in the spirit of organizational performance, but be aware of the resistance you will find and the need to overcome this resistance if norms are violated. For instance, one senior executive was granted "20%" time to explore Future Potential. While this work was meaningful and impacted her decisions at work, it was met with push-back from co-workers, who felt she was shirking her responsibilities and resented the way it impacted her decisions. Communicating her activities to her co-workers, and drawing the link to how those activities might help the business in the future, is one method that could have been used to reduce that resentment. Future Potential explorations, almost by definition, require doing things that are not currently being done within your company. Leaders can prepare their organization for Vitality by creating a culture that accepts these violations of the norms, or at least breaks down some of the resistance.

Fourth, understand the role that "Automatic or Fast" thinking versus "Reflective or Slow" thinking[4] plays in your decision making. Automatic or Fast thinking is when you make decisions in a quick, effortless, and instinctive fashion, with little to no deliberative thought. Heuristics or rules-of-thumb, as described earlier in this chapter, enable this type of thinking by speeding the processing of information and decision-making. Reflective or Slow thinking is when you slow down the decision-making process and consciously think things through. Most of our decisions throughout the course of our day are based on Automatic thinking: These include picking a route to work, or where to grab your morning coffee. Think of it as being on autopilot; you don't need to devote any time to these small, habitual decision. However, if your usual coffee shop did not have coffee one particular morning, and only had tea, you would be forced to think about this particular situation and

---

[4] Kahneman, D., *Thinking Fast and Slow*, (New York: Farrar, Strauss, and Giroux, 2011).

decide what to do next: Drink tea, or seek coffee elsewhere. Your decision-making would be slowed down.

It's one thing to decide your morning drink with Automatic thinking. Unfortunately, too many leaders make big decisions using the same response. The key is knowing when you need to switch to Reflective thinking. As Kahneman once described, a person who is walking will stop walking when asked to multiply two-digit numbers. They have to. That is a natural response to a complex problem. Unfortunately, in the workplace, that type of response does not happen. You need to train yourself to stop what you are doing and focus on the decision at hand.

Making Luck Work for You

Even when you follow best decision-making practices, it can seem like luck—whether you have it or not—plays a significant role. Luck is viewed by various cultures somewhat differently: Some cultures believe luck befalls the deserving, while others believe that luck happens by some external force. In Western cultures, the predominant view is that luck is random, unpredictable, and uncontrollable, benefiting some but not others through no action of their own. Yet there are things you can do to increase the possibility that luck will happen to you and your organization. To cultivate luck, you take advantage of any opportunity, which is especially important when building Future Potential. Here's a good example of someone who made his own luck: A group of MBA students seeking to advance their careers were advised to ask a senior person that they admire in their organization to act as a mentor. Many were hesitant, but one who worked in accounting approached the CFO with this request. The CFO was flattered and accepted, and would occasionally take the MBA student to senior-management meetings for exposure. During one meeting, the CEO asked the CFO a question that he could not answer. The MBA student knew the answer and passed it along to the CFO, enabling him to respond to the CEO's question. As a result, the MBA student became a regular participant in the senior-management meetings. Yes, there was chance and luck involved—it was fortuitous that the CFO did not know the answer to a question—but the student helped create his luck by putting himself out there and asking the CFO to be his mentor. He did not sit back, waiting for someone to discover his brilliance by luck or chance—that's the type of luck that is less likely to happen. The more successful sales people don't sit back waiting for orders to fall from the sky, but rather go out and chase them. You have to make things happen. This isn't limited to individuals; organizations must engage in activities that increase the likelihood that lucky opportunities will arise as they chase the maximization of their performance and the building of Future Potential. The only way to get "lucky" with a new idea, product, or service, is to dedicate the resources to building Future Potential. In other words, you make the odds work in your favor.

Making judgments with heuristics and rules-of-thumb cannot be prevented. They affect everyone, and, as discussed, make managing our incredibly complex world simpler. You cannot attend to every single decision you make throughout the day with the same level of thought or concentration, or else you would be paralyzed by indecision. However, understanding the underlying factors swaying your judgments and decisions will enable you to make better, more informed choices that will differentiate you and your company from the competition.

Assessment: Gauging Your Decision-Making Abilities

Check any of the following items that reflect the reality within your organization or work group:

- We search relentlessly for potentially relevant or new disconfirming—not simply confirming—evidence that our decisions are on target.
- We accept the role in our team of "Chief Contrarian"—someone who tests arguments for why we might be off target.
- We seek diverse, outside opinions to counter our potential overconfidence (e.g., our news and observations does not come from a short list of regular sources).
- We reframe or flip the problem on its head to see if reframing changes our conclusions.
- We avoid the potential for escalation or further emotional investment in faulty decisions engendered by premature "public" commitment.
- The pressure for closure or for agreement with authority on important issues does not overwhelm sound decision-making.
- We devote sufficient time, research, discussion, and attention to major decisions.
- As a group, we have discussed and acknowledged the decision-making biases which put us most at risk.

Decision-making is a complex and varied exercise with both large and small consequences. If you checked six or seven items, then your risk of bias is perhaps manageable. If you checked four or five items, you should spend some focused time evaluating and improving your decision-making approaches. If you checked fewer than four items, you should go back over recent and still-active decisions and evaluate them against new criteria: You may have significant risk. On the other hand, if you checked all eight items, congratulations are in order, but first step back and think deeply as to whether you are biased in your own evaluations of bias. Organizations very rarely are that perfect.

To take this and other assessments online, and get an interactive, customized report, visit OV-CVO.com.

CHAPTER 12

Global Implementation

The Impact of Local Culture

Businesses are increasingly operating on a global stage, and need to consider the question of Vitality not just within the confines of the organization, but across different nations and cultures. As discussed in Chap. 5, certain people naturally lend themselves to Current Performance activities, while others do better building Future Potential. But can this be expanded to apply to a whole group of people from a specific country or culture? Are workers in one part of the world more creative or able to solve complex problems in such a way that it would make sense to task them with Future Potential exploration? Are people from other nationalities less likely to challenge the status quo or to question established procedures to the point where exploration or the tasks associated with Future Potential are fruitless? If so, this might suggest that an approach to Vitality implementation in which different geographies had different responsibilities made the most sense. But are these generalizations correct?

You will certainly experience differences in culture as you travel around the world, and what works well in one business environment might be the kiss of death in another. The Dutch are considered honest and blunt in conversation or feedback, the Chinese deferential to authority, and Americans wary of giving negative feedback without bundling it up with some sort of encouragement or praise. These differences affect how people view one another, and could potentially even cost someone business. Yet, while there is no denying that there are significant cultural differences in how people across the globe act or express themselves,[1] these are superficial distinctions that stem from an individual's particular environment, economic situation, and local culture, rather than any difference in people's innate characteristics. Too often, businesses focus on these differences as inherent to a particular group of people, and use these stereotypes when making decisions. As discussed in the previous chapter, this can lead to bad or wrong decisions. Consider the business executive who complains that the younger generation has no work ethic, or the American CEO who regards his international staff only as a cheap source of labor without tapping into the potential that might exist. As we talk about people, nationalities, and cultures, we run the risk of using heuristics to lump people into categories that they simply and individually don't belong in. For example, women are generally perceived to be less risk-tolerant than men. But one study that looked at the actual distribution of risk tolerance in men versus women showed that male and female risk tolerance is practically the same.[2] If you wanted to find employees for Future Potential exploration with a high tolerance for risk, it would be a mistake to look only at male candidates—something you might do subconsciously. If the job requires a certain level of risk tolerance, you want to hire for that specifically, and not use other measures or traits, such as gender. This holds true for any generalization or stereotype. For example, within the blunt but polite feedback given by the Dutch, it is quite possible to find those who are not blunt or polite. Among the Chinese, who are perceived as giving deference to authority, you will absolutely find those who are less respectful. Historically, the assumed characteristics of national cultures, based on ethnocentric definitions, have been used as inappropriate measures. They seduce because they fit so neatly with many of our rules-of-thumb or heuristics, but they lead to poor decisions.

Rather than putting groups into a box, divided by generation, risk tolerance, country of origin, or any other superficial feature, you would be much better served by focusing on characteristics that the individual possesses and that are critical to maximizing Current Performance or building Future Potential, such as openness to change, creativity, desire to solve for complexity, agility, and resiliency. It is not the broad cultural characteristics or the personal demographics that matter, but rather the skill sets required to operate within each of those domains.

[1] Meyer, E. *The Culture Map: Breaking Through the Invisible Boundaries of Global Business*, (New York: Public Affairs,) 2014.
[2] Nelson, J.A., "Are Women Really More Risk-Averse than Men?" Global Development and Environment Institute, Working Paper No. 12–05, September 2012.

Employee Pride

Visit any Washington, DC, tourist shops and you'll find t-shirts, mugs, and other memorabilia with the names of various agencies emblazoned on them. Tourists parade around collecting all sorts of paraphernalia that say FBI, CIA, Marines, Air Force One, ATF, NSA, and Army, among others. But you will not see one item emblazoned with the initials "IRS," even though it's one of the oldest and most important institutions of the US government. And how does an IRS employee answer the cocktail-party question, "So, what do you do?" With candor, or with an evasive, "I work for the government"?

Feeling pride in where you work is a basic need, and critical for ultimate organizational success. Pride is a universal human emotion. Not only do people want to feel proud internally of who they are and what they have accomplished, but many want to be able to tell others about their accomplishments and bask in a positive-feedback glow, achieving a reflective or relative sense of pride. Pride is different than dignity, which is based on how others treat you. Carrying yourself with dignity, even when faced with adverse conditions, means that you don't react as expected or as others might react. If you were stranded on a remote island and managed to build yourself a clean-water filtering system, it would generate internal feelings of pride, but it would have no impact on your sense of dignity. Whether or not you feel pride in your accomplishments is dependent on your own internal state, while a sense of dignity is externally driven by how others treat you.

We all want to be proud of who we are and what we have accomplished, but like any psychological state, having too much or too little of the characteristic is problematic. Too much pride and you become filled with hubris. Too little pride and you stop caring about important things in your life. As a leader, you want your employees to feel proud of their organization. So how do you achieve that?

First, look beyond senior management. Assessments of organizations invariably show that top leaders feel the most pride in the organization. As you move down through the ranks, pride usually declines, although some organizations are able to maintain high levels of pride throughout. They tend to be organizations whose characteristics include:

- Offering products and services that can be described as paradigm-shifting, innovative, top-rated, industry-dominating, serving a higher purpose, or critical to others;
- Providing clear understanding regarding what the organization is about and what it hopes to accomplish down the road;

- Giving people as much control over their own situation as possible and generally providing more latitude in decision-making, as well as providing what is needed for people to effectively accomplish their work;
- Making sure that people understand they have a future within the organization; and
- Generating feelings of value among staff.

As a result, these organizations are viewed as having effective leadership. Our cocktail-partying IRS employee is likely to be proud to serve his or her country, or see the work as serving a higher purpose. Workers at medical institutions are proud of their service to mankind, helping the ill recover. Teachers are proud that they are preparing the next generation and helping to shape and develop young minds. Sanitation workers are proud that they keep our communities clean and livable. Police and firefighters are proud that they are protecting the public. What drives pride in various organizations is not static. It can change over time. For instance, today people can be proud if they belong to an organization that is operating in a "green" fashion, something that would not have been true decades ago.

People in all different types of occupations want to be proud of their work. They want to take pride in what they do specifically, and what the organization accomplishes. People are proud of what they do, even though you or I may not find a certain job particularly interesting or pride-inducing. People around this world are the same on this: They all want to feel pride, and yet they are all different and can feel proud of quite varied tasks, requiring quite different abilities and skill sets.

When an organization functions in a manner that causes employees to lose their sense of pride, it can be very damaging. Turnover and absenteeism are likely to rise, while quality, customer service, and satisfaction will all decline. Errors will likely increase, and the organization as a whole will start a downward spiral. Organizational performance in general will decline.

Instilling a sense of pride in your employees begins with instilling a sense of meaningfulness, a sense purpose, or a sense that what your employees are doing is important. This begins by laying out a clear purpose for the organization and tying that purpose to the employee's day-to-day job. Help them see the connection. Second, remove job-execution frustration by giving them the tools they need to perform. Third, whatever your product or service is, create a unique strategy around it and strive to have it be the best or best value in its category, with features and capabilities that others lack and are hard to duplicate. Fourth, provide training and developmental experiences for your staff so that they feel good about their skills. Research shows that there are two groups of employees who are most likely to stay with an organization long term: (1)

Those that are being well-trained; and (2) those without skills or whose skills have deteriorated so much that they can't go anywhere else. People who view their skills as slipping, but not yet obsolete, because of a lack of development and training are the most likely group to leave. Fifth, celebrate your accomplishments. Rather than simply conquering one mountain after another without pause, after reaching the top of a mountain, take a moment to open a bottle of metaphorical champagne.

Universal Drivers

While cultural differences certainly exist, they are far too often seen as divisive. Headlines focus on the differences between people and the things that separate us from each other because they are attention-grabbing. News stories abound about generational, national, or gender differences. But plenty of similarities exist between people across this planet, especially in regard to underlying fundamental concerns. Consider the example of a pharmaceutical manufacturing plant in Egypt. A focus group of female quality-control staff—about half of whom dressed in traditional Muslim garb—were asked about what things worked well in the company, and what needed improvement. The reply was unanimous and singularly focused: Eliminate the glass ceiling that prevented them from advancing within the company. This was the exact same response from a group of American women in a similar occupational demographic. The expectations of these women from two very different cultures might vary somewhat, but the underlying needs, hopes, and dreams are the same.

There is nothing unique or exceptional about a desire to improve your lot in life, for it is a characteristic of human nature that is fundamental and global in nature. In fact, most people want the same things out of their working environment: They want to be paid fairly, but they also need to feel as though their work is meaningful, that they are recognized for their hard work, and valued at their organization. They also need to feel that they have opportunities to succeed and advance, and that the company has sound leadership that will enable its success. No matter where you are on Earth, these are the main driving forces. Of course, there are different economic and environmental conditions that affect how these drivers are realized. Employees in India will be paid less than those in upstate New York, who are likely paid less than those in New York City. It is not about making sure everything is universally equal, but rather that it is universally fair. Salaries should allow employees in their own environments to achieve a similar economic lifestyle, yet those salaries will vary widely. This pertains to any type of perk or accommodation that your organization may offer. For example, your US office may allow workers the flexibility to work from home. This perk would be lost in a third-world location, where employees do not necessarily have the necessary technology at home. They might benefit from company-offered transportation instead. The key is figuring out how to make your employees feel valued, secure in their future, and respected within the organization in their various locations. This is achieved most easily when you hire the right local talent who can recognize how best to make their departments or retail outlets run smoothly.

This argument is not limited just to global differences. Today, there is a lot of discussion about how Millennials enter the workforce unwilling to work hard, still holding onto their parents' hands, and expecting frequent promotions. Similarly, younger workers may get frustrated with their older counterparts, who do not see the benefit of flex time or work-life integration. A whole industry of consultants has popped up to teach us how to work together despite generational differences. However, much of what is pointed to as "generational" difference can actually be attributed to life-stage or economic-situation difference. This younger generation does not care as much about job security? Give them a 30-year mortgage, kids in college, and a car payment, and they will care as much as any previous generation, especially in a challenging economic environment. If you create a culture full of mutual respect and reward for good performance, everything else will fall into place. No matter where your employees live, how old they are, or whether they are men or women, they all want to do a good job, feel valued, and feel secure.

Here is proof of this: Tables 12.1 and 12.2 show the rank order of drivers: the factors that cause certain behaviors or attitudes to be more prevalent among a company's employees. Table 12.1 ranks, according to country, the things that make employees feel like they have a promising future at the organization, while Table 12.2 ranks the factors that would cause an employee to consider leaving the company. These drivers are calculated statistically and are the result of large-scale employee surveys conducted across 28 countries. By and large, there are more similarities than differences between individuals from different nations on underlying employee priorities. The same pattern holds true across every company surveyed: People are more similar in terms of their universal drivers than they are different. How they express these characteristics, such as the degree of politeness, the deference to authority, or what makes them feel valued, may differ, but the underlying characteristics are indeed universal. In

Table 12.1 Rank order of drivers of "promising future" at my company by country

Country	Feel like a valued employee	Job options within company	Manager helps me succeed
Australia	1	3	
Brazil	1	2	
China	1	3	2
Germany			1
Hong Kong	1		
India	5		2
Ireland	1	2	
Israel	1	3	
Japan	1	3	
Singapore	1	3	
United Kingdom	1	3	
United States	1	2	

this case, the number-one driver for employees to both feel like they have a promising future at their organization and plan to stay with that organization was "feeling valued," regardless of the employee's country of origin.

Given that this is such an important driver, how do you accomplish it? One way, as already discussed, is to pay employees adequately for the work they perform, creating a sense of equity or fairness. Other potential methods include making people feel that they play an important role within the organization, that their work is helping the organization achieve important goals, that they are recognized for their efforts, and that they have some control over their own destiny within the organization. Employees need to feel that their skills are

Table 12.2 Rank order of drivers of "intent to stay" at my company by country

Country	Feel like a valued employee	Clarity on changes in company direction	Manager helps me succeed
Australia	1	2	
China	1	2	
France	1		2
India			1
Ireland	1	2	3
Israel	1	3	
Japan	1		2
United Kingdom	1	3	2
United States	1	2	8

being developed, that they have a voice that is trusted and listened to, and that they are somehow involved in decision-making. Basically, all employees want to feel included. In "The Inner Ring," C. S. Lewis writes, "In all men's lives… one of the most dominant elements is the desire to be inside the local Ring and the terror of being left outside…. Of all the passions, the passion for the Inner Ring is most skillful in making a man who is not yet a very bad man do very bad things."[3] Lewis was describing the pressures that people feel to belong, and what they are willing to do to get inside the ring of influence that each organization has. This is an issue that plagues many powerful organizations where there is an inner ring of leadership and senior leaders vie both to get into the group and to keep others out. It takes a skilled leader to have that inner ring of influence, but to ensure that it does not thwart the company's Vitality. To prevent it, leaders must communicate their messages throughout the organization, give all employees a chance to be heard, and seek out diverse opinions.

Universality of Labor Relations

By 1896, Abraham Wohlman was a relatively wealthy man. He was living in Belz, Bessarabia, an ancient town with a population of just 6000. Wohlman owned a bookbinding shop, which employed 10 full-time workers, as well as a book store where he sold textbooks and school supplies.

Although he was living with the hardships and restrictions associated with Czarist Russia, Wohlman lived a prosperous life. Married with three children, he was a very warm and compassionate fellow, who was well respected by and a supporter of his community. He had a nice house, with a yard large enough that he was able to keep some cows, chickens, geese, and ducks, as well as to grow vegetables. He treated his 10 workers as extensions of his own family, providing them with wholesome meals at his family's table, which they all shared together.

A new worker at Wohlman's shop would have started as an apprenticeship to a bookbinder at around 11 years old. He would make about eight rubles a month, or 96 rubles a year. (For some context, a small three-room cottage with dirt floors cost about 400 rubles.) Wohlman's workers joined various political parties, and there was a great diversity of political thought among them. It was a dynamic, thoughtful environment, but life was difficult for

[3] C. S. Lewis (1898–1963) was Professor of Medieval and Renaissance Literature at Cambridge University and a Fellow of Magdalene College, Cambridge. "The Inner Ring" was the Memorial Lecture at King's College, University of London, in 1944.

most people; with little food or money it was a constant struggle to survive. Adding to the town's economic woes, anti-Jewish violence was on the rise. In the spring of 1903, the Kishinev Pogrom led to the deaths of 47 people, and hundreds were injured or had their homes destroyed. Czarist authorities did nothing to prevent the attacks until the third day. In October of 1905, a second attack occurred, with 19 killed and 56 injured. (As a result of the first attack, self-defense organizations arose, which limited the number of deaths during the second.) People did not trust the police enough to turn to them for help.

In 1905, as conditions continued to worsen, union organizers came to Belz and convinced Wohlman's workers to join a union that they were setting up throughout the province. The union was pitched as a method by which the conditions of their lives, notably safety, security, and standards, could be improved. One man wrote: "Our shop also became involved in 'the movement.' And six months later a strike was declared. To tell the truth, not every worker was pleased with the strike, because all those who worked for Wohlman respected him and even loved him. He treated the workers like his own children, and not like strangers."

The new union believed that it was not right for workers to eat their meals in Wohlman's home, or to be "treated as his own children." The union demanded a wage increase that would make the workers more independent of that existing feudal system. Wohlman, who was able to provide food for his workers at less cost than what he would have to pay them to buy the food themselves, disagreed. The strike dragged on.

One worker in Wohlman's employ stated, "I can safely vouch that the workers did not enjoy as good a home in their own houses as they did at Wohlman's. It was for this reason that he did not want to pay his workers for their food, since his house was filled with everything of the best, which cost him very little. And so the strike continued ever more stubbornly, so that it became impossible to reach an agreement.... I realized that the strike will not end very soon while the workers were marching around Wohlman's house. Each striker had to find his own place where to stay and a place where to eat. I knew full well the difficult position of my family who, in their extremity, looked forward to my earnings from which even earlier I could not lay aside enough for their needs. And the union could give us no help at all. It simply had no money to pay out, for it had been organized only a short while before. I saw that if I stayed here longer I would soon be left without any money at all. This was my greatest problem at the time. I was sure of one thing; when and if the strike were settled I would again get work at that Wohlman's, since he considered me his best worker and he liked me very much."

While the details of what caused Wohlman's union problem differ from the more common ones today, the underlying issues are absolutely the same. It would be unusual—although not unheard of—for workers today to take their meals with the owner's family as a way to save money on wages. However, the underlying issues that it highlights—respectful treatment, control over one's own destiny, and a sense of equity surrounding pay and benefits—are very common causes of labor unrest anywhere in the world and among any generation. The uncertainty and violence of the times, as well as the poor treatment of the citizenry by those in authority, laid the foundations necessary for fertile union organizing. The strike at Wohlman's, with workers walking the picket lines, lasted approximately one year. It was then settled, with the workers receiving enough of a wage increase that they could choose to eat their meals wherever they wanted. While the strikers did come back to work at Wohlman's bookbinding shop, it is unknown whether they were ever welcomed back at Wohlman's dinner table.

Company Versus Local Culture: Which Wins Out?

Employees will come to your company wrapped in the cloaks of their local cultures. This diversity is important and should be celebrated. Still, there is a need to reconcile significant differences between local and organizational cultures, and there has been a great body of research devoted to it. Sociologist Geert Hofstede first found that strong local cultures had to be taken into account by organizations, and that the resulting management style should be culturally dependent. But Barry Gerhart, professor at the Wisconsin School of Business, re-analyzed Hofstede's data and showed that the differences in an organization's culture can largely be explained not by the country in which the organization is located, but by the policies, practices, and procedures that the company itself adopts. This means that company culture can overpower local culture in many circumstances.[4] One way to determine this is to examine the patterns of variance between employee opinions across organizations globally, to determine whether the amount of variance is greater across countries than it is between companies. In other words, you can use employee survey data to measure whether a company's culture has a significantly higher impact than the local culture, suggesting that an organization's culture

[4] Gerhart, B. "How Much Does National Culture Constrain Organizational Culture?" *Management and Organizational Review* 5:2 241–259.

trumps local culture. Our own data, collected across hundreds of companies and cultures, supports Gerhart's conclusions: Large-scale employee surveys consistently show more similarities between people working at the same company than between people from the same country. In other words, do not get distracted by a country's culture, as your organization's culture will have more of an impact on your employees. As a leader, your role is to understand people's strengths, especially as it pertains to Current Performance and Future Potential, and capitalize upon their unique differences that will help you achieve your company's goals.

Usually, those cloaks of local culture are shed at the door, as employees embrace the customs and values of the organization. You may be located in a patriarchal society with strict gender-based rules, but if your company is pushing gender equality, you will likely find those values within the company. Of course, workplace actions may be different than what you would find if you were to follow your employees home at night, especially in cultures with deeply ingrained beliefs, but in terms of the workplace, you will find more cohesive thinking. And remember, people's attitudes over time will shift to match and justify their behaviors.

To best illustrate this point, consider the globalization of educational institutions. Schools are so ubiquitous that they fade into the fabric of society, and are often overlooked in cross-cultural comparisons. Yet these schools are producing future workers, and helping to shape their views and attitudes about work. In the past 50 years, there has been a radical transformation to global education. In the 1960s, the commonly held notion was that there were extreme differences between educational systems across various cultures. Torsen Husen, generally considered the father of comparative analysis of educational systems, once said, "Any educational system can only be fully understood in the context of the culture, traditions, history, and general social structure of the nation it is designed to serve." This statement is now widely considered inaccurate and becoming more so every day.[5] Today, the prevailing view is that what gets taught and how students get taught is much more similar than different cross-culturally. This uniformity is necessary if the workers of today and tomorrow are to compete on a global stage, and is driven by national leaders who are intent on creating a competitive workforce

---

[5] Baker, D., and Letendre, G., *National Differences, Global Similarities: World Culture and the Future of Schooling.* Stanford University Press, 2005.

in order to increase the standards of living of their populations. Organizations depend upon this uniformity of talent and skills to create their global workforce. That is not to say that sameness rules, but rather that organizational uniqueness should be focused on competitive advantage and not based on misconceptions of local cultural constraints.

Three Variations of Global Organizations

For business leaders, the pressing question becomes how to operate strategically in a global environment where you may have business relationships, offices, or customers abroad. Organizations tend to fall into three categories in terms of how they organize themselves globally. The first is called ethnocentric, where the country of origin of the firm and its culture are considered dominant with respect to all overseas or foreign locations. These organizations develop and improve processes and procedures, as well as invent the future, in their home countries, and then roll them out overseas. The ethnocentric organization makes decisions centrally and in the home-base country. The second type is called the polycentric organization. These are organizations that believe that local cultures are so different that they must be managed by local staff. These organizations will have differing processes and procedures that will likely vary by location and often do not possess a clear global strategy or culture. Decisions here are made by locals within each country in which the entity is operating. The risk that polycentric companies face is that whatever uniqueness made them a success in their home countries may be lost as they expand globally. The third organizational type is geocentric. This is when the organization takes a global view and considers the global objectives of the organization and uniqueness that it offers the marketplace, as well as the local nuances and cultural impacts that will affect performance. Management teams here are multi-national in nature and are selected for their abilities rather than where they are from.[6]

While it might sound like geocentric companies are superior, this depends on the size, scale, and nature of your organization. However, for large organizations with broad and deep talent pools operating in multiple nations, geocentric management styles are generally more successful, because they allow for a more seamless global implementation of strategy and the meritocratic

---

[6] Perlmutter, H. "The Tortuous Evolution of the Multi-National Corporation," *Columbia Journal of World Business*, Vol. 4 9–18, 1969.

rise of top talent. Think of a global hotel brand that offers a uniform level of experience with a unique spin based on local customs that delivers the experience in a way that makes it special. Global uniformity helps companies create a strong brand identity that stretches beyond national borders.

One company (call it "Emerging Global, Inc.") decided to expand into India while installing upgraded manufacturing technology in its US plants. They shipped the older, out-of-date machines, which produced products with wider variation and less precise tolerances, to the new market that they were expanding into. Emerging Global, Inc. may have been focusing on short-term financial savings, but, as you can imagine, it compromised the capabilities of its international operations and the competitiveness of the overseas operation. It made it very easy for competitors who were willing to invest in the latest manufacturing technology to displace them and achieve dominance in the emerging market. Emerging Global, Inc. was maximizing its Current Performance by using the old machines, but minimizing its Future Potential in a way that negatively affected its success. After decades of effort, they have yet to achieve a significant market position in India.

No matter how an organization chooses to operate, the path to success lies in its ability to identify the right individual differences—those things that truly matter in each location in which they are operating—and to couple them with global organizational strategies that are unique, potent, and useful. It is better to manage, mold, and create an organizational culture that will facilitate your success in the marketplace on the global stage than to rely on the often ill-conceived biases of a national culture. The point is to ask the deeper questions and not just spin out strategies and policies around "obvious" personal characteristics or local cultures. The key is to achieve a local adaptation of your global strategies.

As you navigate international environments, it is important to find the right balance between respecting local cultures and implementing your organization's culture. By being aware that the underlying human motivators are universal—the need to be valued, heard, and given opportunities to succeed and advance—you can help your employees reach their fullest potential and help catapult your organization to success. Biases, as previously discussed, exist within us all. Yet we can overcome them by recognizing the similarities that bind us together and celebrating the differences that are special and unique.

Assessment: Global Vitality Potential Assessment

Not every organization has to deal with the challenges of a global footprint. But if your organization is one of the many that does, consider each of the statements below, and check the items that reflect the reality of your organization:

Enhancers

- o My organization is sensitive to local business customs as they concern our customers, employees, business partners, and the local community.
- o If I walked into any of my organizational locations around the world, they would be recognizable and would feel like they belong to the same organization.
- o Each of our organizational locations could be described as vibrant, taking advantage of and celebrating local culture.
- o Employees feel valued, excited about what they are accomplishing, and part of the larger organization.
- o The ideas utilized for the building of Future Potential can come from anywhere within my organization.
- o If someone has a good idea for maximizing Current Performance, they could get attention paid to it no matter where they are located.
- o We find and attract the best local talent in each of our locations.
- o We identity and recognize individuals for the unique talents that they can contribute to our organization.
- o My organization identifies global top talent and places them into positions critical to the organization, regardless of where they come from.
- o In my organization, people get exposure to and are developed for opportunities from a global perspective.
- o The building of Future Potential in my organization happens in many locations across our enterprise.

Derailers

- o My company operates uniformly across the globe and does not adapt to any local needs.
- o There is little that differentiates my organization from other local organizations in the countries in which we are located.

○ There is no uniform look, feel, or culture across our global organizational locations.

○ We try to find good local talent, but it is just are not available in many of our locations.

○ There are stories circulating in my company about the shortcomings of locals in the various countries in which we operate.

○ Senior management positions in overseas locations of my organization are filled by employees from the home country.

○ Expatriate senior managers tend to lead according to the standards and practices of their home countries rather than local standards.

Give yourself a +1 score for each Enhancer you checked, and a −1 for each Derailer, and add them together. If your total score is less than +4, you have some clear work to do in managing the breadth of your enterprise. If you scored +5 or more, you are well on your way to operating in a broad and global fashion.

To take this and other assessments online, and get an interactive, customized report, visit OV-CVO.com.

CHAPTER 13

Storytelling

Van Halen and the Brown M&Ms

What is the power of a story?

Rock-and-roll band Van Halen is known for its diva-like demands. The big-haired, spandex-clad band members, led by singer David Lee Roth, hit their peak in the 1980s. But before getting up on stage to throw some of the most staggering rock concerts ever, with unprecedented stage intensity and pyrotechnics, they would contractually demand that a bowl of M&M candies be placed in their backstage lounge—but a bowl with all the brown M&Ms taken out. The band would throw a fit whenever the bowl of candy in their dressing room had brown ones in it. A full-blown, rock-and-roll, trash-the-place tantrum. At one Pueblo, Colorado venue, David Lee Roth destroyed his dressing room, including kicking a hole in the door, which ended with itemized damage he called "twelve thousand dollars' worth of fun."

This is a powerful story of terrible rock star behavior. Heard this way, you'll have an explicit and likely unfavorable image of the band in your head.

But here is another story. This is about Van Halen, a rock-star band unlike any other that had come before. This band performed some of the first megaconcerts, staging an incredible show with amazing pyrotechnics that was as much fun to watch as it was to hear. But these shows were arduous to produce. The stage sets were hugely complex, with intense electrical and structural demands. Mistakes could result in show mishaps, delays, or—as happened in Pueblo, Colorado—a faulty judgment about the weight tolerance of the stage that caused damage costing up to $85,000. Even worse, collapsing beams or electrical overloads could hurt people. Before Van Halen, the typical rock band hauled around three tractor-trailers full of equipment. Van Halen's concerts required *nine* tractor-trailers.

With so much stuff, how could you ensure the set-up crews, different for each town, read the specs correctly? Van Halen had an ingenious solution: Buried deep in the contract, in Article 126, was a simple clause that all brown M&Ms must be removed from the bowl of candy in their dressing rooms. As the band arrived to check the venue, a quick check of the M&M bowl was a reliable predictor of other mistakes. This would trigger a line-check of the entire production to find the guaranteed technical errors.

This story, told two different ways, has very different results. Rock-band brats or business geniuses? This is the power of a story.

The Power of Organizational Storytelling

Storytelling is integral in today's business world. Stories connect and help us share ideas, goals, and values. Stories captivate, educate, and inspire. Within an organization, stories bind people together, humanize top leaders, and motivate employees. The culture of your organization is shaped by the stories people tell when you are not in the room. Over the past decade, storytelling has been increasingly formally recognized as an important part of organizational life. Storytelling has inspired leadership research, consultant businesses, and even the job title of "Chief Storyteller." But it has always been important.

Our brains are wired to make sense of the world in terms of narrative. Stories work with, instead of against, the cognitive shortcuts and heuristics we use to make sense of the world. Stories are easier to remember than facts and figures, and easier to retell, helping the availability heuristic, which, as mentioned in Chap. 11, is the inclination to rate as more probable those cases that come more easily to mind. The conjunction fallacy, the tendency to give more weight to detailed explanations than to simple ones, is essentially the same as giving more weight to a "story" than to a simpler concept. Or survivorship bias, described in Chap. 7, which refers to, drawing conclusions from examining only successes, rather than contrasting successes to failures, and which also represents the very human, very strong response to stories. While it is absolutely important to educate and develop resistance to cognitive biases, it can be similarly important to embrace this part of human nature and to acknowledge the power of storytelling by using stories to your advantage in communicating the leadership messages surrounding Vitality priorities. Especially important are stories about times when failures and learning from mistakes were embraced. The goal of these kind of stories is to encourage others to explore Future Potential, and not shut down risk-taking within the organization.

Compelling narrative transports us into the action. Rather than stepping back and critically evaluating the message, we step into it and ride along with the storyteller. We love origin stories, like how Les Wexner, founder of Limited Brands, borrowed money from his aunt on the sly in order to open a business and prove a point to his dad: Namely, that some of the most profitable items in an apparel store were "limited" to the lower price-point basics, like socks and underwear. And triumph stories, like how the value of Post-It Notes was met with skepticism until the clever inventors got 3M's own administrative assistants hooked… and then cut off supply. And stories that reflect values, like how one executive summed up an expensive mistake by saying, "I have just invested $10,000 in your personal development. Learn from it."

But we also love the trainwreck stories, those that tell of disaster, intrigue, thievery, and general nastiness. Around an organization's hallways, you may hear about how those using bribes were caught as they tried to close a business deal overseas, how an executive fell down sloppy drunk in the men's room at a convention and cut his forehead on the sink, or how errors were ignored because accuracy would take too much time. These stories move us because they humanize our leaders by suggesting that they are either fallible or great, or serve as dramatic examples of our leaders' ethics, which determine whether employees respect and trust them. Some stories expose the repugnant aspects of a business, and may be powerful enough to cause change. Regardless of whether they are good or bad, the best stories are authentic, and catapult us to a greater understanding of the people running our organizations.

Stories happen whether you want them to or not. People use them to make sense of organizational events, whether they are good or bad. As seen with Van Halen, events can be spun in myriad ways. Trying to control the stories told about you or your organization is like trying to control what goes viral in the Internet: It is mostly impossible. But you can learn, not only how to tell the stories that are constructive to the organization's strategy and future, but how to frame them so that others will tell their own versions that will help drive the organization forward.

Telling Stories from Data: A Primer for Scientists

Stories illuminate data. They make it easier for the listener to understand and remember data. But it takes a special kind of storytelling to convey the message of research, whether the message has a scientific or metrics-based foundation. The implications need to sweep beyond the original technical experts. If you are one of those technical experts, here are a few tips on how to tell stories from data:

1. **Do not undermine validity.** Define the conclusions as if you had to defend them to a panel of critical colleagues, sharing the technical foundation of your message.
2. **Consider your audience**. Your listeners are likely to have different backgrounds and come from different disciplines, and they may not accept the same technical foundations that drive your message. They will require a different kind of evidence, perhaps evidence that you would personally not find compelling, such as examples and single cases, rather than statistical coefficients based on rigorous methodology.
3. **Start with a relatable message**. As you craft your narrative, start at square one and rebuild your conclusions based not on your technical approach, but from a storytelling perspective. TED talks almost always begin with a personal story to connect the storyteller with the audience. This may mean banishing all of your presentation slides with statistical coefficients to the appendix, or a completely separate reference document, and rebuilding the slides from scratch. It may double the effort, but without it, the impact will be lowered by more than half.
4. **Drive your audience toward action**. Bulletproof cause-and-effect relationships are virtually non-existent in pure science. In the language of science, research can "support" or "fail to support" hypotheses. Yet for the lay audience—those who may make decisions based upon your work—leaps of faith beyond the strict evaluation of a hypothesis will need to be made. Help guide your audience toward the best conclusions with causal assertions when necessary, taking care to understand that being completely definitive is unnecessary.
5. **Draw upon evidence beyond the current project.** Your audience will not make decisions based solely on your report. You will need to understand and incorporate evidence from beyond your current project in order to address the full spectrum of concerns your audience might have.
6. **Deliver an engaging story.** Data alone will rarely inspire or drive action. Marketing a technically based product or idea depends on a different discipline and skill-set than developing the product or idea in the first place. Facts and figures might make you seem smart, but stories will make you compelling.

The Discipline of Storytelling

Many people say they would tell stories if only they knew any good ones. But, as described by Ira Glass, host of NPR's storytelling program *This American Life*, "Stories happen to those who can tell them." In other words, it is not the quality of the story but the ability of the storyteller that matters. A good storyteller can spin a yarn around any event, engaging listeners about even the most mundane experiences. Learn how to tell a story, and the content will emerge.

You can learn how to become a compelling storyteller. Start by finding a compelling message you want to share. Focus on your audience: A story told to senior leaders will resonate differently than one told to lower-level employees. Make sure you tell your story in your own voice. As a leader of a vital organization, the story must be true, because authenticity is fundamental to getting your message across. Otherwise, the stories that others will tell about you will revolve around your insincerity and lack of integrity.

Veteran Hollywood filmmaker Peter Guber distills the lessons of his industry into truths of storytelling for the business leader,[1] starting with the idea that stories are not just about entertainment, but about instruction and action. Organizational storytelling is, according to Guber, "a force for turning dreams into goals and then into results." The vital organization can use storytelling to help realize the promise of Future Potential and the ability to convert it into Current Performance by following his four key pieces of advice:

1. **Truth to the Teller:** As discussed, organizational stories must be authentic and true. They should be consistent with the storyteller's values and style, and the basic message of the story cannot change in subsequent versions. As Guber says, the storyteller's "tongue, feet, and wallet must move in the same direction." The act of storytelling can be difficult for some, because it requires vulnerability on the part of the teller. Some of the most potent stories we tell and retell are about decisions that cost us money, but pursue some value that is more important, like employee safety or integrity with customers. Conversely, we also focus on the stories where leaders seem to be giving mere lip service to a value, when their budgetary decisions seem to reflect another narrative. Employees often never know top lead-

---

[1] Gruber, P., "The Four Truths of the Storyteller," *Harvard Business Review*, 53–59, December 2007.

ership directly. Not all leadership's actions are observed, or all their decisions explained, but stories can help make them accessible. To illustrate, a president of a health-care delivery organization in the southeast USA once expressed dismay at low employee-survey scores regarding whether management used good employee ideas. She said, "They just don't know how much they keep me awake at night." That simple statement drifted out of the conference room and into more general awareness. It helped to flesh out a human side to the president, which credibly reflected this truth.

2. **Truth to the Audience:** For stories to be effective, they need to resonate with the audience and draw them into the message. The storyteller needs to grasp where the audience is coming from, and how to identify with them. Guber tells of Sallie Krawcheck, who held CEO positions at Smith Barney and a Citigroup unit, as someone who could easily have intimidated audiences with her brilliance. Instead, she drew them in by citing the common bond of awkward preteen years, saying, "There was nothing they could do to me at Solomon Brothers in the '80s that was worse than the seventh grade." Contrast that style with another president of a professional services firm, who tried to connect with his audience by talking about the "cash" the organization had accumulated and had available to devote to various business-development efforts. What the audience actually heard was the disconnect between the rich organization and the low wages they were paid. Leaders commonly tell their stories of confidence in the future based on their own sense of market forces, spreadsheet-based metrics, and intimate decision-making sessions, but the most compelling stories of the future must start with what the audience, not the top leaders, values and cares about. The leader who talked about cash should have started by talking about the efforts of employees, and the success that earned. Then he could have talked about how that enables investment into new realms of Future Potential.

3. **Truth to the Moment:** For stories to be gripping and compelling, they need to feel genuine at the time. Clearly, many stories will be told and re-told, and will not always be spontaneous. Even if you have heard a story before, when a great storyteller recounts a tale, you have the sense that it is not verbatim from a script or a regurgitated reflex, but is powered by a passion genuine in that moment. In these cases, the power of the story is multiplied. We are immediately grabbed when a leader starts with, "I had a prepared speech, but I am going go off-script," because it feels as

though something genuine and of-the-moment is coming. This kind of agility in storytelling is a skill that can be developed. Paradoxically, while storytelling should seem to come from the heart and not from rehearsal, it still requires discipline and preparation. Think of the popularity of so many TED Talks, which begin almost formulaically with a personal story before launching into potentially very sophisticated or technical topics. It may be a formula, but it works. Listening to TED talks, whether they are relevant to your field or not, can help you understand the techniques of good storytelling. Less work-related but no less fascinating are stories from The Moth, a non-profit organization dedicated to the art of storytelling. At Moth events, storytellers stand live before an audience without notes, making the tellers vulnerable as they convey a "Truth to the Moment" story.

4. **Truth to the Mission:** Lastly, the story must echo something larger than that one story or storyteller. This happens when it is clear that the leader is devoted to a cause larger than him or herself. Origin stories told by founders are so compelling because the launching of a business (or a product or service) is synonymous with the entrepreneurial passion to create something amazing that that did not exist before. And that creation is so often the story of an underdog beating the odds, or of an ingenious duct-tape and paperclip solution that worked. To hear the emotional backdrop that predates success helps to tie the leader to the organization and its mission, and motivates the audience to participate in continued success. Clearly, not all missions are success stories, and not all tellers are part of an origin story. But the devotion to something larger than oneself is compelling in the telling.

Not all stories will be grand, sweeping narratives to auditoriums of willing audiences. But these same truths apply even on a smaller scale. For smaller snippets of stories, here are some tips to enhance compelling imagery:

1. **Cultivate use of the metaphor.** Metaphors help people understand concepts on a new or deeper level, and move into new and creative extensions of the original idea. Often, creating organizational change requires communicating sophisticated concepts from diverse fields, like finance, statistics, technology, or global trade. Finding the right comparison to something familiar to your audience can cut through technical barriers to

enable them not only to understand, but to contribute. Use a cliché or two if you must to help you get started. However, clichés fall completely flat when used as a crutch and are not fully embraced. To help you keep sharp, ask your audience what their hobbies are, or special interests—cooking, horseback-riding, or water polo—then try to illustrate your points. Even the old cliché of "keeping your head above water" will certainly have a deeper resonance to a water-polo player. Try metaphors that are true to your passions as well, but in the spirit of exploring Future Potential, accept that not all attempts will succeed. Learn what works, use it, and cultivate the sensibility of continuous experimentation.

2. **Quote some greats.** Being careful of overuse, and, never as a justification, but as a way to draw people into a topic, keep an eye out for well-phrased aphorisms from sources that make one think more deeply about the words. Below are some quotes from other disciplines that invoke aspects of Vitality:

   - Logic will get you from A to B. Imagination will take you everywhere. *Albert Einstein.*
   - Great art picks up where nature ends. *Marc Chagall.*
   - There is no science without fancy and no art without fact. *Vladimir Nabokov.*
   - Science is what we do to keep us from lying to ourselves. *Richard Feynman.*
   - How many legs does a dog have, if you call the tail a leg? Four. Calling a tail a leg doesn't make it a leg. *Abraham Lincoln.*

3. **Try for a little suspense.** Definitely do not annoy people with artificially inefficient communication. However, "We made four million dollars on that deal," while impressive, may not convey the deal's drama. Imagine instead the executive, his worn leather chair creaking as he leans forward, recounting how he narrowly missed his flight home and was stuck overnight in China. The beautiful, spacious hotel where he spent the previous few nights was fully booked, and he was lucky to get a room at a run-down inn owned by a local couple who fed him a traditional Chinese meal. The executive details the delicious food, explaining how he overcame the language barrier to communicate with the husband and wife well enough to learn that they wanted to sell their inn. He tells the story of buying the inn and turning it into a first-rate hotel and ends, with triumph: "We made

four million dollars on that deal, all because I just missed that first flight." Clearly, this story will have a greater impact on the listener than hearing that a new hotel in China made four million dollars. While you cannot embellish your stories with fictional details, spend some effort to notice and convey the details that make the imagery more memorable for the audience, giving the main message more impact. Sensory details particularly transport the listener into the story (note the word "creaking" in the micro-story above). If there is a place for it, smell, though the least used, is the most compelling sense to invoke in storytelling.

4. **Avoid melodrama.** Suspense is not the same as artificial drama. Melodrama in a business setting is a description of everything as urgent, critical, a "must win," or "burning platform." Organizational leaders often fall into the trap of manufacturing urgency out of fear, rather than out of compelling opportunity. Particularly in the marathon race of sustained exploration into Future Potential, leaders need to set challenges that inspire passion rather than anxiety. Consider President Kennedy's 1961 speech to the United States Congress to ask for the money and commitment to put a man on the moon, delivered during the uneasy period of the Cold War. Despite the rampant fear, his speech focused more on excitement than on fear. He concludes by saying, "New objectives and new money cannot solve these problems. They could, in fact, aggravate them further unless every scientist, every engineer, every serviceman, every technician, contractor, and civil servant gives his personal pledge that this nation will move forward, with the full speed of freedom, in the exciting adventure of space." The nation's exploration passions were ignited by the compelling and audacious goal, and not by the fears or anxieties of a "burning platform."

5. **Share the character arc.** In literature, if the protagonist demonstrates no personal development from the beginning to the end of the story, the personal impact on the audience is lost. Big stories stem from major character change, and, in turn, change us. Reveal how people have changed, what they have learned, and the epiphanies you personally have had. To the extent that you want your stories to change others, it makes sense to start by sharing how they have already changed you.

As your stories are told, found, or fostered in others, the most successful ones will embody the above features of classic storytelling. Elaborate upon them in order for your stories to have impact.

There are any number of sources for finding and crafting your own stories. Consider what is important to you, and keep alert to examples of where those efforts or values are illustrated in both good and bad ways. Consider organizational activities, current events, history, television programs, classic literature or drama, and personal experience. Some find it useful to have a file for gathering stories, including relevant organizational events or actions by individuals. Throughout this book, we have used stories, illustrations, and metaphors from 3.3 million years ago to the present day. We have cited examples from business, wildlife conservation, and wildlife itself. We have leveraged personal experiences as well as widely known examples. And we have done so to help convey the important points of Vitality in a way that will resonate with you and stick. The key, as Dr. Seuss reminds us, is that, "From there to here, and here to there, funny things are everywhere."

The kinds of stories that are often told in business settings include:

- How We Started
- The Nature of our Challenge
- The Striving-to-Improve Story
- Emblematic Success Stories
- Performance Tales
- How the Organization Took Care of Employees
- Where We Are Going

Each of these stories can contain messages of Current Performance, Future Potential, or a blend of both. As you tell yours, or hear others tell stories, pay attention to underlying Vitality messages.

Telling Compelling Vitality Stories

Stories of Future Potential within organizations tell of how new capabilities are developed. They expand the definition of the business you are in by pushing the boundaries of new possibilities, yet stay within the strategic frame. True to the nature of exploration, not all are success stories. Sharing business failures helps to encourage the right kind of risk, and can help inoculate against the frustrations of failure. These stories help to battle the "villain" of day-to-day pressures, which are mainly the distraction of Current Performance, which prevent devoting energy to Future Potential. These stories keep minds open to explore new ideas, and remind us of the need to lift our heads above the daily grind to look around with fresh eyes. They can be very exciting for all employees, even those not devoted to exploration, as they talk about what the organization can be in the future.

Stories of Current Performance are about winning and an often controlled and systematic pursuit of a specific goal. They can be about individuals or teams who work through a known challenge to outperform either their own history (one for the record books), another group, or an external competitor. The tale may be about the core business, making money, saving costs, or saving time. Sports analogies abound here, with players on a known field, with established rules, and a way to keep score. Importantly, stories of Current Performance should remind us that the adventurous excitement of Future Potential should not overshadow the elegant virtue of expertise and getting things done.

In addition to those two kinds of stories, there need to be stories of Vitality that illustrate the interplay of exploration and execution. These stories tend to cover a bit of both Future Potential and Current Performance. They can unfold over time, as with a product-lifecycle story where the inspirations of exploration become systematized into the execution of a well-oiled machine. They might potentially detail how that machine eventually needs transformation to something new. They can also instruct us in the ways Current Performance and Future Potential efforts coexist among us, potentially as different parts of each of our jobs, helping us shift from execution to exploration and back again.

Table 13.1 gives some examples of how these different stories will vary from one another. There will be overlap among the three basic types: Current Performance, Future Potential, and Vitality. Not all stories will be individually complete narrative arcs. Some will be snippets or scenes. Some will be metaphors chosen to illustrate. Some will be more complete "fireside chats." Yet the collection as a whole will reflect your strategy and set the frame for how people think about who you are today and want to be in the future. They can be cautionary tales, origin stories, or illustrations of values. They help integrate into the social fabric of the organization the ways in whicht you define success, the ways you might achieve it, the pitfalls to avoid, and how you will know when you are on track.

Table 13.1 Examples of storytelling

Storytelling element	Current Performance	Future Potential	Balance of Vitality
Basic Plot	How we earn money	How we develop new capabilities	How we balance execution with exploration
Heroes	Champions	Explorers	Boundary Spanners or teams of both champions and explorers
Conflict/Villain	Inefficiency, competition	Day-to-day pressures and failure to explore; risk of failure	Execution and exploration in isolation, not valuing each other
Resolution	Performance against goals or plan	Learning something new	Cycles of exploration that lead to execution and back again
Message/Values	Streamlining the established; virtue of execution and expertise	Exploring the new; risk-taking; excitement of what we can be	How we adapt, survive, and evolve over the long term

Picasso's $100,000 Napkin

What is the value of a product or service? Often, leaders look at a confusing blend of time, cost to deliver, and sense of value to the recipient when setting prices. But ultimately, the price is what someone is willing to pay—or what someone will accept.

Consider this story about Pablo Picasso, who, while enjoying an evening meal at a restaurant in Spain, was interrupted by a diner who set a cloth napkin down on the table. He asked, "Could you just sketch something for me? I'll pay you for it. Name your price."

Picasso took a charcoal pencil from his pocket made a rapid sketch of a goat. It took only a few strokes, yet was unmistakably a Picasso. The man reached out for the napkin, but Picasso did not hand it over. "You owe me $100,000," he said.

The man was outraged. "$100,000? Why? That took you no more than 30 seconds to draw!"

Picasso crumpled up the napkin and stuffed it into his jacket pocket. "You are wrong," he said, dismissing the man. "It took me 40 years."

Had the man paid for it, how much do you think that napkin would be worth today?

The Stories Others Tell

Everyone is full of stories, from top leadership down to the lowest-level employee. And no matter where you stand on the rung, it is critical to listen. As a business leader, it is your responsibility to set up an environment that promotes the stories that help drive the organization forward.

Here's a good example of a business leader who, in recognizing the importance of listening, helped create a new story as well. Masa Tanaka, when President and CEO of Union Bank, kept a giant rubber ear in his desk. As a Japanese expatriate running a US company, he knew he needed to stay calibrated to the voices of employees. Often, when an employee came to speak with him, he would pull out the rubber ear and, holding it up to his own ear while maintaining a serious demeanor, would cock his head and open his eyes a little wider as if he were listening intently. He used his big rubber ear to make the point that he understood that he needed to listen. Importantly, he was not just listening but also reminding other executives that they needed to listen as well. In the process he created a lasting image in the minds of others that prompted *them* to tell stories: *Have you seen Masa's ear?* Stories always abound about CEOs, regarding what they do, what they value, and who they are. Masa helped shape the stories told about him. What do you want your employees to say about you?

Research shows that people who tell stories are more committed to the organization.[2] While the research has yet to pin down this chicken-and-egg question, it suggests that the stories told tend to be more pro-organization than anti-organization. It also suggests that you can nudge the effort by helping those committed employees to tell their own stories.

First, listen to the stories your employees have to tell. Develop the routine of asking for their stories. Ask about how Current Performance is improved. Ask about how Future Potential opportunities are recognized and pursued. Question them about the balance inherent in becoming Vital. Retell the stories that help promote the messages valuable to the organization. While listening to everyone is important, keep in mind that the most potent stories will come from those with broader audiences. These storytellers tend to be respected and motivated Boundary Spanners, usually with longer tenure in

---

[2] McCarthy, J. F. "Short Stories at Work: Storytelling as an Indicator of Organizational Commitment," *Group & Organization Management, 33(2),* 163–193, April 2008.

the organization. More than that, they tend to have developed the storytelling discipline. So identify them, and listen.

Second, develop storytelling discipline within your organization. Simply asking employees for their stories is a start. Beyond that, encourage the use of stories, metaphors, allegories, and other narrative devices. Organizations that depend on effective cascading of information down the management ranks will often have meetings or briefs to tell middle managers the messages that need to be passed along. Use those venues as opportunities to share not just the facts, but the stories you expect middle managers to share with their people.

Third, increase awareness of the fantastic happenings within the organization that demonstrate the organization you want to be. Beyond that, create the events about which others will naturally tell stories. Organizational symbolism is important here. One organization established the Lame Duck Award, which rewarded grand failures in innovation. The prize went to those who did all the right things—ventured into the unknown, pursued an important organizational goal, took risks and experimented with new approaches, or learned important lessons—but who were unable to succeed. The point was not to highlight failure but to reward the effort in order to encourage persistence in developing Future Potential. Another organization going through a dramatic transformation wanted to underscore the changing mindset required for the future. In a dramatic fashion at a town-hall meeting, all the top executives had collected scraps of paper inscribed with practices they themselves and others around them were pledging to stop. These were ceremoniously thrown on stage into a coffin, which was then paraded out into the parking lot and burned. Was that by itself enough to transform the organization? Of course not. But it set up the stories and conversations that made the task easier.

Other than anchoring symbols such as lame ducks or coffins into organizational lore, audacious events will spawn their own stories. The Blitz Day described in Chap. 6 is one example, where a health care organization approached every employee who came to work in single day, instructing them to come up with an idea to improve patient care or customer service. This large-scale action spawned stories for years to come. The stories were about care, service, innovation, and the large organization's ability to move into the future. Even more audacious, in 1978, after two of his EDS executives were taken hostage by the Iranian government, Ross Perot tasked retired Colonel

Bull Simons to assemble a team of highly decorated Vietnam veterans from EDS's own workforce to rescue his people from a prison in Tehran. Perot did not need to tell that story, or highlight Truth to the Teller, Audience, Moment, or Mission. It told itself.

There is no question that you will want to tell your own stories. The real impact, however, is in the stories others tell when you are not in the room.

Final Imagery

Imagine that Van Halen front man David Lee Roth was like a corporate CEO, surrounded by a hyper-vigilant set of vice president-like staff bent on supporting their leader's vision. Understanding its importance, this staff might pay special attention to reinforcing the contractual M&M rule. Over time, and driven by his well-meaning staff, it would be easy to picture how Roth's M&Ms would take on a life of their own, disconnected from the original purpose and becoming an end unto themselves. The counting of candy does not have face validity as an effective metric of operational compliance. In the stories the organization would tell of its leadership, the underlying genius would fall away and the diva image would become a reality for lower-level employees. After all, criticizing leadership is easy. And sometimes a little fun. Thus, misunderstanding would endure. How many other metrics, rules, or decisions have also become ends unto themselves?

Rock stars are not required to explain themselves. In fact, maybe the mystique is greater if we are all left to wonder a little. This quickly becomes problematic for CEOs or other leaders. Make sure to tell the stories that keep the organization focused on the right messages of Vitality.

Assessment: Evaluating Your Vitality Stories

Your own discipline and climate for storytelling can be evaluated by checking the statements below that reflect the reality of your organization:

- ○ Stories, examples, illustrations, or metaphors about how your organization improves itself come easily to mind.
- ○ There are told and re-told stories that are about Current Performance—streamlining, cost control, or other improvements to the ways things are already done.

o There are told and re-told stories that are about Future Potential—exploration, breaking new ground, and developing new capabilities.

o People re-tell the stories they hear from leadership, with similar messages being emphasized.

o Stories told by the leadership of your organization are credible and resonate with the audience.

o You consciously look for and develop stories you can tell that relate to organizational improvement or other aspects of what is important for the future. (Some of these will be your re-telling of stories that other leaders tell.)

o You actively cultivate the storytelling discipline within yourself.

o You foster constructive storytelling by improving the discipline in others or creating dramatic symbols or audacious organizational events that spawn stories in others.

If you checked six or more items, then your storytelling discipline is better than most, and this is a tool in your toolbox to help improve Vitality. You will be well-positioned to foster the storytelling discipline in others. If you checked four or five items, you should spend some focused time listening for stories and building your own discipline. If you checked fewer than four items, you may not have previously considered the power or storytelling, and should find one or two instances you might match to your strategic agenda.

Whatever your score, as you address these questions, think of a new story about either Current Performance or Future Potential that you can tell. Experiment. Try new approaches. Get started tomorrow.

CHAPTER 14

Step-by-Step Guide

Taking Stock

You now have the advice, the tools, and, we hope, the motivation to implement the Vitality Model within your own organization. Perhaps you have been following some Vitality principles already, whether by design or by instinct. Regardless, organizations that are successfully operating in a vital manner will have three elements of their approaches in common: They will base their approach on clear strategies that differentiate them from the competition and provide an advantage; they will generate meaningful insights into how their organization is running through both rigorous metrics and informed judgments, and they will take inspired action based on their strategy and insights. These three components create a continuous feedback loop that enables you to tweak your strategy based upon insights generated and actions taken (see Fig. 14.1).

Strategy, insight, and action are the three fundamental elements of an empirical or evidenced-based approach to organizational improvement.

If you are just embarking upon your Vitality journey, you may be wondering where to start. Noted executive coach Steve Temlock would encourage you to start by asking three basic questions:

- Are you spending your time doing the right things?
- Are you doing what you need to do in order to win? (The ambiguity of this question is purposeful, as those things depend greatly on the executive's particular field.)
- How would you spend an extra hour every day, if you had one?

Fig. 14.1 Strategy, insight, and action

Temlock can anticipate the bulk of responses. His clients feel as though their days are jam-packed with meetings, putting out fires, or just attending to other day-to-day issues that don't allow them to ever focus on the larger, Vitality-related issues necessary for long-term success. By asking clients how they would spend an extra hour, Temlock makes them think about how they should be spending their time in order to move their business forward. Temlock's clients need to shift their daily priorities and responsibilities in a way that provides them with an opportunity to think strategically, communicate their message and vision, and achieve the overarching balance of Vitality. If your own answers to Temlock's questions mirror the answers he often receives, it may be time to re-think your approach to the business and to re-invigorate it by implementing a new paradigm based on the principles of Vitality. This approach works whether you are running a not-for-profit organization, a government agency, a small pizza shop, a daycare, a national finance company, or an international conglomerate.

The first step in taking stock of your organization is to think through each of the six key elements depicted in the Vitality Model (see Fig. 14.2).

For each—Leadership, Employees, Processes, Offerings, Service, and Customers—you should be able to outline your efforts around both Current Performance and Future Potential. Take a moment to evaluate your own

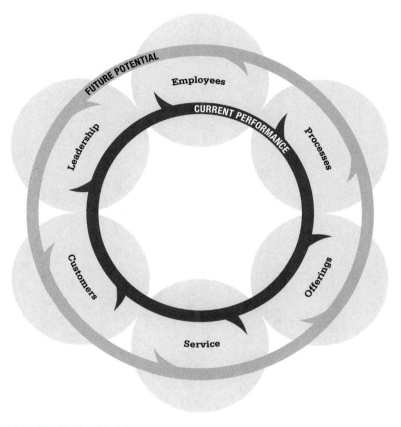

Fig. 14.2 The Vitality Model

organization on Worksheet 14.1. Step back and squint, and you will find overall patterns that give you a sense of how your organization is doing. Give your organization a letter score of A, B, C, or F on performance in each of the twelve evaluative areas. Then take a step back once again and look at the column. What score would you give your overall organization on Current Performance? On Future Potential?

Once you have identified where you need to focus improvement, it is time to make the necessary changes in order to implement a Vitality culture within your organization. Keep in mind that CEOs and other organizational leadership cannot do this alone; the organization must be brought along on this journey. The next step involves creating your Vitality plan, educating others to its importance, and understanding the reactions of your employees to your plan.

Worksheet 14.1 Rate your organization's Vitality balance

	Current performance	Org score on Current Performance (A, B, C, F)	Future potential	Org score on Future Potential (A, B, C, F)
Leadership	Leadership is sound with the right leaders in the right positions to achieve effective execution; it rewards execution of existing plans.		Leadership is spending time envisioning, inventing, and communicating the future; it rewards efforts to step back and develop potential.	
Employees	Employees are thriving and highly performing in their respective areas, having the necessary skill sets, training, tools, and environment for performance.		The organization attracts plenty of highly talented people and can retain the best; it experiments with developing new areas of competence.	
Processes	Internal and external procedures are efficient, innovative, high quality, and have effective cost control.		Internal and external procedures are agile, allowing for continuous adaptation and improvement.	
Offerings	Offerings to our customers are attractive, with products and services that are currently in demand.		We have a healthy "pipeline" of new offerings the marketplace will find attractive in the future.	
Service	Our customer-service orientation and support systems are exceptional; customers feel great when interacting with the organization.		We are building our brand with effective marketing, sales, and brand management; service approaches are agile in adapting to new offerings or new customer needs.	
Customers	Our customer base is well-defined and loyal, with high levels of cross-selling, up-selling, or repeat business.		Our customers are brand advocates to others and are excited about any new products and services we roll out; we explore new marketplace segments.	
Overall Grade				

Plan, Educate, and Understand

Implementing a Vitality culture is, as with any cultural-change effort, both a top-down and bottom-up exercise. As you approach a culture-change effort or a change in direction for the organization, senior leadership can debate and argue among themselves, but what must emerge from those discussions is a unified vision that is presented to the rest of the organization. To encompass Current Performance and Future Potential, the vision should include those things that you "must" be good at in order to serve your current customers well and run your organization in an effective and profitable manner, as well as those things that you "can" be good at. These are, most notably, the things that will enable the organization to thrive over the long term.

Begin to plot out your own personal vision of the Vitality future for the organization by completing Worksheet 14.2. In this chart, describe one area of improvement for at least three or four areas of the Vitality model, or, if you want, all 12. These are areas that would make you a more vital organization if you improved upon them. You can ask each of your direct reports or peers to complete this chart as well, and then compare visions and opportunities seen, as well as which opportunities may have the largest positive impact on the organization in group discussions. A facilitator for these discussions can often help keep them on track and generate the most useful outcomes.

An organization's culture is not driven solely top-down or bottom-up, and the implementation of cultural change, while it must start at the top, must be supported by those up and down the ranks. If an attitude of "this too shall pass" emerges, the attempt at Vitality will fail. If some groups or departments don't support the changes and operate as "guerilla groups" within the organization, they can do great damage to the implementation of a Vitality culture. As a result, it is important that buy-in is universal.

The next step in planning, educating, understanding, and, importantly, in achieving the buy-in of all employees is to conduct what is called a "pre-mortem," which is a technique that assumes that the changes you are envisioning have already occurred and failed spectacularly. Though not an absolute prerequisite, a pre-mortem can be very useful and prevent missteps. The pre-mortem technique is based on 1989 research by three professors, Deborah J. Mitchell, then at the Wharton School, Jay Russo of Cornell, and Nancy Pennington, then of the University of Colorado. They found

Worksheet 14.2 Identifying areas for improvement

	Current Performance	Description of improvement (or indicate none if satisfactory)	Future Potential	Description of improvement (or indicate none if satisfactory)
Leadership	Leadership is sound with the right leaders in the right positions to achieve effective execution; it rewards execution of existing plans.		Leadership is spending time envisioning, inventing, and communicating the future; it rewards efforts to step back and develop potential.	
Employees	Employees are thriving and highly performing in their respective areas, having the necessary skill sets, training, tools, and environment for performance.		The organization attracts plenty of highly talented people and can retain the best; it experiments with developing new areas of competence.	
Processes	Internal and external procedures are efficient, innovative, high quality, and have effective cost control.		Internal and external procedures are agile, allowing for continuous adaptation and improvement.	
Offerings	Offerings to our customers are attractive, with products and services that are currently in demand.		We have a healthy "pipeline" of new offerings the marketplace will find attractive in the future.	
Service	Our customer-service orientation and support systems are exceptional; customers feel great when interacting with the organization.		We are building our brand with effective marketing, sales, and brand management; service approaches are agile in adapting to new offerings or new customer needs.	
Customers	Our customer base is well-defined and loyal, with high levels of cross-selling, up-selling, or repeat business.		Our customers are brand advocates to others and are excited about any new products and services we roll out; we explore new marketplace segments.	

that prospective hindsight—imagining that an event has already occurred—increases the ability to correctly identify reasons for future outcomes by 30%.[1] Here is a basic approach to conducting a pre-mortem for a Vitality discussion[2]:

- Step 1: Bring your team together. This should be made up of those employees who completed Worksheet 14.2.
- Step 2: Describe to them the implementation of a Vitality culture in the organization, including what steps you would want to see taken and the hoped-for outcomes.
- Step 3: Tell them to imagine that one year has passed and the plan to implement a Vitality culture has completely failed. It is now seen as a complete and total waste of time.
- Step 4: Ask each assembled person, independently, to write down the various reasons which they think could be the cause for the failure. Give the group exactly five minutes or so to do that, which gives people enough time to think it through, but not enough time to focus on anything except top-of-mind issues. The independent work is also critical, as each person will then use their own world-view and decision-making heuristics.
- Step 6: Go around the room and have each person contribute one potential cause of failure. Create a master list at the front of the room with everyone's ideas. Keep this up until all potential causes of failure have been listed.
- Step 7: Vote. Tell each person they can vote for the three most likely causes of failure from the master list generated. No need for a paper tally—a show of hands is fine. Count the votes up and see which issues are viewed as the top three critical risks. (People can cast all three of their votes for one issue if the feel that strongly about it.)
- Step 8: Discuss how the implementation plan can be modified to address the top concerns to assure that they don't happen.
- Step 9: Other, lower-down priority issues can also be addressed later on in further discussions.
- Step 10: Re-visit the list periodically to assure that the failure points are still being mitigated as you proceed with implementation.

[1] Armbruster, S., Moran, J.W., and Shirley, J., "Pre-Mortem Analysis," Public Health Foundation, July 22, 2014.
[2] Adapted from Gary Klein, *The Power of Intuition: How To Use Your Gut Feelings To Make Better Decisions At Work.* (Doubleday, 2004).

Why is it necessary for the cultural change to happen both top-down and bottom-up, or to go through the steps to achieve buy-in? An organization's culture starts at the top, and it is only there that broad policies and practices that have a big impact on creating a culture can be set. However, these changes must be accepted by the rank and file for the culture to actually shift. To achieve the necessary buy-in up and down the line, an educational effort needs to be undertaken, starting with obtaining the support of those at the top of the house and then moving down through the ranks. Don't skimp on the time it takes to do that. Once the senior leadership team is on board, plans can be put into place regarding the Vitality structure of the organization, and those plans can be part of educational efforts for lower levels.

Structure

As highlighted in Chap. 6, there is a distinct benefit to organizational structures that place some separation between the teams and business units driving Current Performance and those building Future Potential. However, this is only true if the separate Future Performance groups maintain a clear and direct connection to top leadership and the organization's overarching strategy and priorities. As highlighted in Chap. 6, whatever the organizational structure and the attempts to provide buffers from day-to-day concerns, the broader lessons are these:

1. Create a buffer from the day-to-day realities so that those involved with developing and implementing Future Potential can focus without distraction from those realities.
2. Maintain the right executive-level sponsorship and involvement to stay connected to organizational strategy and priorities.
3. Enable the right kinds of boundary-spanning to cross-pollinate, share resources, and stay calibrated with the most important stakeholders.

It is the latter two points that ensure that, over time, the original structural separation that fostered the new product, line of business, or approach becomes integrated into day-to-day functioning. This can be a critical junction, which is often prone to failure. Electric cars, which many consider to be the Future Potential of the automobile industry, will ultimately succeed at scale only if they can deal with the inconveniences of the time it takes to charge them and the need to find a charging location, as well as the reluctance of car dealerships to promote a product that may ultimately mean less profitability for them.[3] The uniqueness of the car and its physical separation from the mainstream driving experience must change over time. If charging stations were integrated into the existing infrastructure of gas stations, and if the charging pit stop took no longer than the time to fill a gas tank, the success of electric cars would be virtually guaranteed. Solve the additional problems of cost to produce, drive, and maintain, and the market demand will quickly skyrocket. Integration of the new product, service, or business into existing structures allows for greater leverage from existing infrastructure and organizational resources and processes. Future Potential morphs into Current Performance.

Structural separation can be costly, and not every organization can afford that approach as it builds Future Potential. A more cost-effective manner is to enable structural separation on a personal level. For instance, a manager might find herself working on Current Performance issues for the vast majority of her time, but might block out time on the calendar each week to work on Future Performance opportunities. This is the notion of the 20% time that is set aside from an employee's daily tasks. It is just one of many techniques that some companies have tried in order to foster innovation and creativity.

Other factors that will affect your structural decisions include what kinds of products and services you provide, the size and geographic footprint of your organization, the location of any centers of excellence, whether you have a large number of units (like a restaurant chain), the ability to deliver a uniform product or service globally, and a host of other factors.

Structural separation divides the organization into units, with some focused on Current Performance and others devoted to the exploration of Future Potential. This means that different departments or units within the organization have different goals, objectives, time horizons, and abilities to evaluate their work. The benefit of this approach is a clear focus in each department on its objectives and an understanding about how its success will be determined. However, the development of Future Potential then runs the risk of being something that happens "somewhere else," and not the responsibility of those who are close to day-to-day production or service-delivery processes. Additionally, the inherent tension between the maximization of Current Performance and the building of Future Potential is increased as

[3] Richtel, M., "A Car Dealers Won't Sell: It's Electric," *New York Times*, Nov. 24, 2015.

employees tasked with one or the other compete even more for the limited resources available.

A traditional approach is a structure that makes no special allowance for separating the work of maximizing Current Performance from the building of Future Potential within the same organizational units. The benefit with this approach is that everyone feels that they have the responsibility to move the organization forward. However, potential lack of focus risks poor performance in the present, as people are distracted by future-development efforts, or jeopardizes the building of Future Potential, as these needs may be delayed due to the pressing daily realities of Current Performance.

The tension that exists between these approaches is a challenge that every organization must deal with, and which should be thoughtfully assessed and solved depending on the organization's unique characteristics. Whichever path you choose, you must simultaneously build resiliency and agility into your organizational structures. Table 14.1 summaries the benefits and challenges associated with these approaches.

Table 14.1   Structural separation versus traditional approaches for creating Vitality

Approach	Pro	Con
Structural separation	Clarity of focus for the Future Potential groups Deep specialists developed Coordinated approaches can be rolled out More easily scalable Special projects can be better kept secret and secure	Financial costs of slack and redundancy, additional support systems and structures Lack of collaboration between Current Performance and Future Potential Unresolved paradox of balancing Current Performance with Future Potential More difficult to keep separate groups focused on organizational priorities
Traditional approach	Knowledge-transfer or sharing between groups Easier transformation of Future Potential into Current Performance Increase in resiliency through bench strength and cross-training Enables new ideas from across the organization instead of just a specialized group; improved short-term financial performance due to less redundancy	Generalists without deep knowledge Current Performance trumps building of Future Potential Higher cognitive load for people tasked with both Current Performance and Future Potential responsibilities On-going maintenance of keeping Current Performance and Future Potential integrated and balanced

Ultimately, structure should be determined based on the pros and cons that are otherwise hardest to manage. Once the structure—or structures—of the organization are decided upon, it is then possible to determine how to cope with the "cons" of your selection. Part of that will be based on which individuals best fit specific roles. This may be as simple as clarifying roles and expectations, or it could require more extreme change.

Staffing

Upward Movement. Positive Change. Renewal. These are enduring themes that get our personal attention, and they apply to organizations as well. The employees with the greatest confidence in their employers and leaders do not necessarily come from the largest or most successful companies, but rather from organizations seen as having the best prospects or brightest futures. They are organizations with positive *directional* change, and they are building Future Potential as they simultaneously achieve a high level of Current Performance. Organizations lacking in these areas, regardless of size, have more negative and less confident staffs.

Putting into place those leaders and employees who can achieve high levels of forward movement in both Current Performance and Future Potential is critical. Not everyone is suited to both, and most cannot do both well. Who will be your pioneers, and who will keep the lights on day-to-day?

Your three big buckets of talent will fall into Executors, Explorers, and Boundary Spanners. Most people within your organization, if your organization is already serving customers, will by necessity be Executors. These are the folks who keep the place running day-to-day. They are your "factory," which generates today's revenue and profits. They are selling, marketing, analyzing, accounting, making inventories, manufacturing, quality-checking, delivering, servicing, and interfacing with your customers. They need to be doing this all in an effective and efficient manner. Your Explorers are usually a much smaller group than the Executors (perhaps with the exception of start-ups). They are researching, inventing, designing, and re-invigorating. They are looking into new approaches and new markets and lines of business. The organization can develop and nurture these Explorers in-house, or can purchase their work products by acquisition. Finally you have those who can operate as Boundary Spanners. These are people who can either move between execution and exploration, or can operationalize those things that your Explorers develop, transitioning Future Potential into Current Performance.

Think of the critical positions within your organization. Complete Worksheet 14.3 by circling the characteristics that fit for a few positions in your organization that deliver on Current Performance, and then do a few for positions that are working on Future Potential. Finally, see if you can identify any Boundary Spanners and see if their characteristics match the definitions below. In which column does each one tend to fall? Does the person in the position fit the description? Can you describe your executive team as a group operating in a Vitality fashion, balancing the characteristics of the Executor, the Explorer, and the Boundary Spanner? Worksheet 14.3 helps you identify which employees fit these specific categories.

Worksheet 14.3   Staff positions according to Vitality role

Position:_____	Executor characteristics	Explorer characteristics	Boundary Spanner characteristics
	Able to deliver a consistent, high quality existing product or service to customers; customer-service focused.	Able to learn from existing environment and transform it into something new and innovative	Operationalizes new products and services into market-ready, reliable, reproducible, and cost-effective products and services
	Laser-focused on targets and goals (e.g., sales, cost control); exceptional attention to detail.	Makes targets and goals secondary considerations, shifting them as new avenues and opportunities arise and explored	Determines and understands market potential for new products and services as well as opportunities; determines worthwhile investments; recognizes fail-fast moments
	Embraces consistency, excellent manager, motivates and develops team, drives exceptional performance	Embraces change, adaptable, self-motivating, never satisfied with current products, methods, or procedures	Experienced, knowledgeable, can deal with ambiguity, and can take changes of the Explorer and see how to integrate into Executor's day-to-day operations

While putting those with the appropriate skill sets and abilities into place throughout the organization is critical, it is just as critical to implement and integrate a plan that puts the balance of Current Performance and Future Potential at the top. When your senior team gets together, there should be advocates for Future Potential-type issues as well as champions of Current Performance topics. Each advocate needs to realize the importance of balancing and achieving both sides of the business, rather than being driven only by their own specific needs. To ensure proper focus, it is helpful for major issues to have a specific representative on the senior management team. For instance, if technology is a bottleneck and needs to be upgraded in the organization, there should be a CTO/CIO-type person on the senior team who is focused on and advocates for that issue.

Implementation

As we discussed, most organizational change requires elements that will change dramatically and other elements that will shift in a more incremental fashion. Changes in structure and staffing need to be done in a way that keeps the organization's heart beating, allowing it to continue to function on a day-by-day basis by servicing its customers, manufacturing its goods, or producing its services. It must be able to pay its bills, onboard new staff, and execute on other critical functions. Institutional memory needs to be maintained and transferred as any new staff get put into place.

With all those realities taken into consideration, you can develop a step-by-step plan for moving toward Vitality. This chapter represents a rough outline of how such a plan might unfold. As you implement your plan, remember that there are three critical components to keep in mind (see Fig. 14.3).

First is Message, which shares the rationale and motivation driving the change, as well as explaining employees' roles during and after the transition. Second is Performance, which involves making sure that employees are given the tools they need to carry out their tasks, whether they are related to Current Performance or Future Potential. Third is Future, which means illustrating for employees both the company's long-term Future Potential and their own individual ability to thrive within the organization. When all three pieces are in place—Message, Performance, and Future—employees are more likely to support the change and feel motivated to contribute to its success.

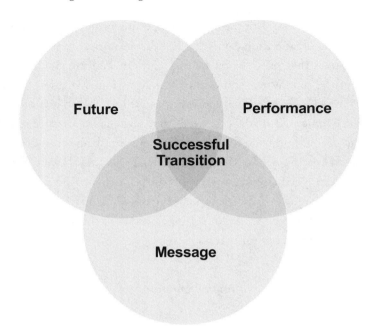

Fig. 14.3 Message, Performance, and Future

To ensure that all three aspects are present, ask yourself:

1. What is the message that you will be delivering to employees about the prospective change? Does it outline a strategy or just state a goal? Is it motivational to the average employee? Does it depict how you will be maximizing Current Performance at the same time that it describes the Future Potential?

2. How will you enable performance in the new environment, assisting employees to make the change from the current state to the new state? Will additional training, tools, or other resources be required? Is staffing adequate for any new procedures or processes? Recognize that there will be a learning curve: Performance at the start of the process will likely not be the same as when new processes and procedures are well-established. Will recognition and reward systems need to change to support desired outcomes?

3. How will you assist employees in seeing a future for themselves in the new or changed organization? Does the organization enable them to see a direct line between what they are doing and the organization's strategy and goals? Will they feel that their skill sets are obsolete? Do they feel like they have a career and do they feel valued?

Work Towards Achieving Balance

The Vital Organization is one that is performing well on both Current Performance and Future Potential. And in order to do that, both aspects of performance must be supported within the organization. If the focus is solely on Current Performance, specifically on running lean and profitably, you might be generating lots of cash, but at the expense of your future. And if your main focus is on Future Potential, your lack of cash and Current Performance will make it harder to achieve the envisioned future. As you consider where to put resources, consider the balance that must be struck. Understand that there is tension between these two goals that must be continuously resolved and re-balanced throughout the organization. You are aiming for the upper right quadrant of the Vitality Matrix which necessitates a simultaneously high level of both Current Performance and Future Potential (see Fig. 14.4).

As you evaluate, if you find that the organization is too focused on Current Performance at the expense of building Future Potential, it may be that your structure or your staffing needs to be tweaked. Perhaps processes need to be re-engineered, or better training on execution given to staff. Without that Future Potential component working well, you may survive for a while, but the long-term future prospects for the organization are not positive. And if all you are working on is Future Potential, you will likely not last long enough to get to that future. Balance is crucial.

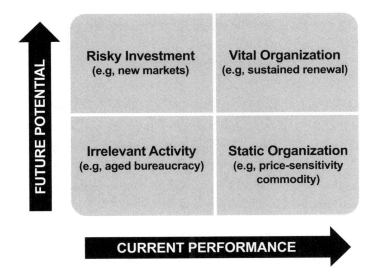

Fig. 14.4 The Vitality Matrix

Table 14.2 Evaluating agendas for Current Performance versus Future Potential

Current Performance issues	Future Potential issues
Operational matters such as workload, production, or delivery	Threats to the organization, such as new competitors, environmental disruptors, or economic conditions
Lack of pricing power for the goods and services your organization sells	New opportunities and capabilities, such as developing new markets or business lines
How to hit financial targets	Product, service, or resource investments
How to streamline ways you are already doing business	Product or service re-vamping or renewal

Think back on the last few meetings your management team had to discuss operational issues and talk about where the company is going. Table 14.2 will helps you evaluate overall agendas at such meetings according to whether they fit into the Current Performance or Future Potential side of Vitality:

At this point in the book, you should already know that the senior management group must operate in a Vitality fashion by focusing simultaneously on the maximization of Current Performance and the building of Future Potential. While most time and attention will likely be devoted toward Current Performance, perhaps even 80%, you will need to step back and ask whether you have the right opportunities to develop Future Potential in order to achieve your overall strategy. If your meetings are slanted toward one or the other, you need to re-balance by designing meetings differently, and setting specific agendas that focus on the areas that are lacking.

Evaluation

We often seem to base our assessments of various kinds of situations and organizations not on absolutes, but on how the situation and the organization are changing. Are they moving in a positive direction, or are they stagnant or in decline? People are drawn to organizations that seem to be in the ascendency, and rapidly abandon even relatively high-performing organizations that are seen to be in decline. This appears to be true not only for employees of organizations, but for customers as well.

So the starting point for the evaluation of your Vitality performance should be assessing the goals for improvement and monitoring carefully for any decline. Develop measures that will inform you if you are on the right path toward the simultaneous goals of Current Performance and Future Potential. Current Performance is generally easier to measure, with easily understood metrics like costs per unit, sales performance, scrap rates, or number of accidents. Measuring Future Potential is tougher. Some metrics might be product-refresh rates, patents, product pipeline, or growth from new product lines or first-time customers. But going beyond "hard" metrics will be required. Ask yourself: What is the level of confidence that senior management has as a group regarding the direction the company is headed? How excited is the sales force about the new product pipeline, and do they see opportunities to cross-sell new products into the existing customer base? These are all measureable by assessing sentiment utilizing strategic surveys. Some of these measures might be empirical, others will derive from professional judgment, and some will come down to informed leaps of faith. Worksheet 14.4 summarizes some possible metric choices for Current Performance and Future Potential. It is not necessary to evaluate your status using all of these methods. Rather, focus on the critical few—the one or two metrics that are focused on the four or five areas of Current Performance and one or two areas of Future Potential that work best for your organization. Check whether you have any evaluation methods in place already or if you need to develop them, or mark unneeded methods as not applicable.

If during your evaluations you find that all is not working as you envisioned, make changes. Always remember that it is imperative to fail fast. If something is working, do more of it; if it is not, try something else. A vital organization should be thought of as ever-evolving, but with a rationale. Change for the sake of change is nothing but chaos, but change and refinement that have solid rationales should not be shied away from. Stagnation is the antithesis of Vitality and continuous refinement can help to keep stagnation at bay.

Tell Your Stories

Stories can be very powerful in shaping and communicating organizational norms and culture. People use them to interpret, understand, and guide their behavior. As we discussed, the skills to learn are not just about telling stories that are constructive to the organization's strategy and future, but also about how to set a frame within which others will tell their own stories to

Worksheet 14.4 Measuring Current Performance and Future Potential

Vitality Challenge	Sample metrics of Current Performance	In place, develop, or N/A	Sample metrics of Future Potential	In place, develop, or N/A
Leadership	Revenue production, output, or budget performance of leader's department, 360 or upward feedback scores for execution-related dimensions		Leadership bench strength, 360 or upward feedback scores for exploration-related dimensions, investment	
Employees	Evaluation of workforce competencies to produce employee engagement, safety incidents, voluntary turnover		Projections of future workforce headcounts, climate for innovation, global competency, resilience/adaptability	
Processes	Resources per unit of production, customer delivery systems		Agility for adapting production lines to new products	
Offerings	Market share, comparisons to competitor products/ services		Product pipeline, new markets/revenue streams	
Service	Service standards, up-sell/cross-sell rates		Service climate/orientation of employees, alignment of multiple service channels	
Customers	Customer satisfaction with existing products/ services, re-purchase (or defection) rates, switching costs		Customer relationships, brand image, sales pipeline within emerging markets, agility for moving into new territories/segments	

Worksheet 14.5   Crafting your Vitality stories

	Current Performance	**Future Potential**
Positive story		
Cautionary tale		

help drive the organization forward. The stories people tell from within an organization are one definition of culture. Stories illustrate, direct, motivate, transform, and educate. Storytelling is so powerful a mechanism that it has become heavily researched with respect to its impact and most effective use by leadership. As you implement Vitality, begin to build your catalog of stories that can become part of organizational folklore. Stories of Future Potential within organizations tell about the ways that new capabilities are attempted. Stories of Current Performance are about winning in an often controlled and systematic pursuit of a specific goal. Worksheet 14.5 will help you get started crafting your stories. Write a positive one for both Current Performance and Future Potential. Is there also one for each that is a cautionary tale? Something that illustrates a violation of norms or standards within the organization and how this was dealt with?

Reward Milestones

One way to build resiliency into the organization is to reward the accomplishment of milestones. Milestones may be either organizational or personal accomplishments, such as successful completion of goals. Recognize a job well done, an obstacle overcome, a significant task being accomplished, or the obtaining of significant new knowledge, skills, and abilities. Companies achieve this by installing robust reward and recognition systems. Providing people with recognition of achievement is a worthwhile investment.

Without recognition of achievement and rewards, the never-ending piling-up of goals and tasks to be accomplished can grind employees down and leave them wondering why they put up with it all. After all, if you never can see light at the end of the tunnel, how do you know if you are actually moving in the right direction?

- List a few of the major rewards your organization has in place to incentivize and recognize Current Performance. Are they matched to the right people/jobs and are they well-matched to Current Performance achievement?

- Now list a few or the major rewards you have in place to incentivize and recognize Future Potential. Are they matched to the right people/jobs and are they well-matched to Future Potential achievement?

Do you reward the attempt/effort, or just the outcome? Do you reward significant milestones in performance improvement? Do you reward those things that actually support your strategy and goals? Are you actually rewarding the things you espouse—the things the organization says it stands for—or merely providing lip service?

Don't Stop: Be Relentless

Organizations need to improve constantly and raise the bar of performance, both in terms of the products and services they offer and how their employees view the organization. Simply maximizing Current Performance by having the best product or service out there, or by being an attractive employer, is just not good enough. Rather, seek a longer-term, evolutionary path of constant improvement, which requires building Future Potential in order to achieve long-term organizational health and employee motivation.

The ideas and the vision of senior leaders need to become widespread throughout the organization. Relentless and visible commitment by the top leadership team to the duality of Vitality—the simultaneous pursuit of Current Performance and Future Potential—is critical to overall success and disseminating that vision.

Dogged, systematic, and relentless pursuit of your goals is required for actual attainment. Senior-management leadership in this area gives the organization plenty of opportunity for modeling to occur, so that others within the organization can see what Vitality looks and feels like. Seeing how senior managers practice Vitality will help inform them about what is expected of them.

CHAPTER 15

The Path Forward

Chances are, you have specific hopes and dreams for your own organization, even for your specific team, or, importantly, for your own career—what you stand for, what you can build, and what you want your legacy to be. Working today and building for tomorrow is what Vitality is all about. But it will be fueled by your own passions—what you care about and what drives you. The best way to start your path toward Vitality is to identify what drives you forward.

You might be motivated like some of the people referenced in this book. Think back to the MBA student, mentioned in Chap. 11, who had the gumption to ask someone to act as his mentor and wound up invited to participate regularly in executive-level meetings. Consider the small group of community members who re-invigorated their local farmers' market. Or Gary Stich, CEO of Oxbo, who manages his annual business cycles according to Vitality principles. And then there's Cristián Samper, head of WCS, who is saving the elephant one small valley and one poacher-turned-farmer at a time. Like them, you too can enact meaningful change. Start by focusing on the "one thing" or "critical few" issues that will be most meaningful to your own efforts, even if not your entire organization, and move forward from there.

Other business books may promise you a quick fix, or "10 easy steps" to be successful. This book does not promise you that. Like any good diet or investment plan, there is no magic solution that comes without discipline. The path to Vitality takes hard work, resources, and a relentless commitment to constantly seek Current Performance improvements while simultaneously developing Future Potential.

Why travel down this road? Today's global economy is full of opportunities, but success can be fleeting, as customers are fickle and new products and services are constantly developed and brought to market. Whether your organization survives and thrives depends on how efficiently it can maintain its Current Performance, while simultaneously exploring Future Potential possibilities. Whether you are a CEO of a start-up or international conglomerate, a business student looking for your first job, or an individual somewhere in between looking to grow a business, the tips and tools in this book will help you transform your existing organization—or even just your work group—into one that thrives not just in the present, but in the future as well. Leaders all want the same thing for their organizations: sustained success. But the way often gets muddled. We hope the tips offered in this book, based on decades of research and experience, help highlight the best way forward.

Many of you are likely already focused on both Current Performance and Future Potential because elements of it "feel right" for your business. They feel right because in many respects they represent common sense. But the power of common sense, as we pointed out in Chap. 11, is greatly enhanced by going beyond simply making sense of the world and moving to a place of true understanding as well. For the uninitiated, this book represents an eye-opener. For those who are playing around at the edges of these concepts, this book offers concrete tips that can be used for long-term success. And for those who are operating squarely within the Vitality paradigm, this book represents a confirmation that you are on the right track. All of you can leverage the concepts and techniques found here to improve your organization's performance.

Cycling Between Future Potential and Current Performance

Current Performance works until the pressures of the marketplace or business directions demand transition, forcing your organization to pursue various Future Potential opportunities, which comes with both risk and failure, as opportunities are explored, attempted, and abandoned, until you reach that breakthrough innovation that transitions into your Current Performance. And then the cycle starts again.

Sustained evolution requires managing the cycles of exploration and execution. Perfectly adapted, maximally efficient Current Performance systems are the enemy of developing Future Potential. If calcified into a bureaucracy without the passion, agility, or directive to try new things, an organization's approaches will anchor it in place and become obsolete as the world changes around them. There is an active tension between success in Current Performance and success in Future Potential. A constant press into a tightly focused domain of Future Potential is vital. While there may be milestones to evaluate progress along the way, the ultimate judge of Future Potential investments is when they are converted into Current Performance. The natural progression is when what used to be breakthrough innovations are eventually created more cheaply, based on established systems and procedures. This will happen most elegantly when the leaders of Current Performance systems are sufficiently co-ordinated with the leaders of Future Potential development, and can effectively plan with one another how to adapt.

Through these cycles, what is your role? Do you streamline Current Performance in order to keep the operations of the business humming smoothly and making money? Do you envision the Future Potential of where the organization can go? Are you the type to convert Future Potential into Current Performance? All are required. All have virtue. Any can be your legacy when they are connected together in the language of Vitality. The specific domain of your legacy will depend on your job. As alluded to throughout this book, your challenge might be to develop Vitality within yourself or other individuals, within the team, or within the organization.

Vitality Within the Individual

As individuals, we have all felt the challenge—and the frustration—of trying to be Vital. The press of deadlines, the demand of customers, the flow of a manufacturing line, or even the efficiency of well-established procedures will all keep us anchored to Current Performance approaches and keep us from developing our Future Potential aspirations. "I don't have enough time" is a universal refrain. Virtually a mantra for some, it is equal parts both a truth and a cop-out. We are rarely truly without choices in how we spend our time. If you do not have time for something, you are prioritizing something else instead.

The good news is that Vitality is a learnable discipline. The first requirement is to develop the "growth mindset" (see sidebar, Chap. 5) that the balance of Current Performance and Future Potential can indeed be improved. That belief—that faith—that Vitality can be improved will enable growth to happen. Even in our most hunkered-down, Current Performance-execution days, there remains a bit of the Future Potential Explorer in each of us. Find that Explorer spark and build some structure around it. Label it, set aside time for it, create some nudges, and align it to what your personal mission is within your work.

Remember, this will be a struggle for you as an individual. You will attempt things and you will fail at some of those things, perhaps many of them. Failing at an attempt is not the failure of the process, or a failure of the framework, but a sign that a different direction or concept might need to be pursued. Be resilient. Don't fall into the trap of assuming that a failure will lead to a negative cascade of events—a concept called Catastrophism—in which you think one set-back will set off a chain reaction of failures. Embrace failure as part of the Vitality process; it provides an opportunity to learn, grow, and discover which behaviors, processes, or procedures need to change for your next attempt to be a success. Don't give into the fear generated by a failed attempt. Rise above it!

Vitality Within the Team

Your team of individuals each brings to the table different strengths to create Vitality. Get to know them. You might be lucky enough to have "Boundary Spanners" on your team. These are the individuals who manage to succeed with tasks that both streamline Current Performance and develop Future Potential. You might set up goals, support systems, offsite activities, or recognition programs to develop how each employee might devote effort both to execution and exploration. It is also true that you might not demand that all your employees be equally competent in both execution and exploration. Your group may contain individuals who at various times specialize. You might assign execution- or exploration-related activities to different people. Within the strategy you set, the stories you tell, and the ways you set the stage for improvement, your team will appreciate the value and the integration of Current Performance into Future Potential.

Vitality Within the Organization

If you lead a larger function or organization, the stakes are higher, yet you will have more tools at your disposal to create and maintain Vitality. You will have more freedom to play with organizational structures, systems, metrics, or other evaluations of success, and, of course, overall strategy. With this freedom comes the burden of ambiguity, uncertainty, and risk. You will define what business you are in, what makes you unique, and how you will focus your Future Potential efforts on expanding that uniqueness into the future. Critically, you will shape the agenda of your executive team, and can mold them with a relentless focus on Vitality.

Embrace the Chaos

The process of becoming Vital will be an organic, often chaotic, sometimes meandering path that is unique for any given organization, division, or work group. There are frustrations when our aspirations are virtually guaranteed to exceed our grasp. There are human foibles and biases in play, made riskier as we work across an increasingly global marketplace of customers, ideas, suppliers, and employees. The complexity of it all can be daunting.

However, the best advice to maximize your odds of success is to be proactive. Finding your way to Future Potential requires experimentation and the agility to try and re-try new things until you land on not just what works, but what works *and* furthers your strategy. Agility without strategy can be destructive. The world is hard enough. Efforts should be directed to overarching guidelines regarding what makes you unique.

Keep yourself honest. Train yourself to become aware of human foibles and biases, as well as both the myths and realities of the global marketplace. Develop metrics and other systematic ways to evaluate your progress. Honor the very real differences between Current Performance and Future Potential.

However you find your Vitality path, it will help to surround yourself with a team who can talk, debate, pound fists, and eventually align toward a vital balance of Current Performance and Future Potential. For you, your team, and your whole organization, define the message for how you will connect day-to-day operations with long-term vision. Just as The Wildlife Conservation Society can redefine the algebra in the Luangwa Valley from short-term prosperity based on illegal poaching to long-term sustainability of both the farming villages and the African elephants, so too can you set the stage, tell the story, and implement the plan to inspire Vitality within your own domain of influence.

One final tip, based in behavioral economics: Set up a monthly recurring meeting with yourself and at least one other person. This person can be your boss, a mentor, a peer, or any other person with good ideas about how your group can evolve in the future. The broad agenda will be to discuss the development of Future Potential and how to integrate it within your Current Performance. Other tasks and to-dos will come, potentially based on the previous chapter's more complete set of suggestions. But commit to this now and create the recurring meeting.

Creating a vital business is not easy, but the effort you invest now will pay off in the long term by positioning your organization to adapt to any threats or changes. Today, your business may be focused mainly on the day-to-day pressures of Current Performance. But now you understand the need to constantly look toward the Future Potential, to be unafraid to try new things, and even to fail sometimes, because even that failure is valuable. You now have the tools to transform your organization from one that is merely surviving to one that is thriving. This is your Vitality journey, your potential to create a legacy that will outlast you: Embrace the hard work and enjoy the opportunities ahead.

APPENDIX A

Complete Vitality Self-Assessment

At the end of each chapter, there are a series of questions to help you anchor the main concepts in your own work, and to evaluate your organization or your own tendencies to operate in a Vitality fashion. Those questions are gathered together and adapted in this appendix as a convenient way to understand and evaluate the Vitality environment—in terms of both strengths and opportunities—in which you find yourself. You can also go to OV-CVO.com for a more complete and rigorous evaluation, along with an interactive report unique to you.

These assessments, especially when used in conjunction with the worksheets and steps in Chap. 14, can help suggest where and how to focus in order to become a more vital organization or to increase you own skill set in the area of Vitality.

As you work through the items for each chapter, feel free to answer with your whole organization, your business unit or division, or even your department in mind. Vitality is a concept that applies at all levels of an organization. It is also applicable to other types of organizations of which you may be a member.

Chapter 2: What Is Vitality?

Chapter 2 describes the broad concept of Vitality, tells why it is important, and sets the stage for subsequent chapters to dive more deeply into various aspects of balancing execution and exploration in your organization. The first broad question asked is: In your organization, do you focus on streamlining

Current Performance—squeezing more output from your resources, shaving costs, or pressing for speed—or do you step back from the day-to-day and consider the future of your business/organization, including what kinds of products and services your team or business need to provide in the future? Following up on this question, and reverberating through the rest of the book, there are other questions to challenge you, such as: How do you balance Current Performance and Future Potential? How well do you build Future Potential in order to stay relevant over the long term? As those Future Potential ideas and innovations emerge, how effectively do you convert them into efficiently executed Current Performance machinery in order to please current customers, create needed cash flow, and stay in business or functioning as an organization?

The following statements below will help you structure your answers to those questions, and help you frame your own thinking as you read the rest of this book. For each of the statements below, check the items that reflect the reality of your organization:

- We excel on Current Performance metrics dealing with efficiencies like speed, efficiency production, service ratings, cash flow, and profitability.
- We have a healthy Future Potential "pipeline" of products and services we are experimenting with or have under development that will keep us relevant, competitive, and unique in the future.
- More than 50% of my organization's products or services have been refreshed or introduced in the last five years.
- My organization is able to balance gracefully the competing needs of executing and streamlining Current Performance, while simultaneously exploring and building Future Potential.
- We effectively share resources across the organization from successful Current Performance in order to fund efforts to build Future Potential.
- Over time, we effectively convert Future Potential ideas and innovations into streamlined execution that delivers Current Performance.
- Our company has demonstrated the ability to grow without sacrificing the quality of what we deliver.
- I have confidence in the future of my organization.

Give yourself one point for each statement that you could clearly and unhesitatingly check. If you checked seven or eight items, then your Vitality discipline is better than most, and you will be well-positioned to leverage even the more advanced concepts in this book. If you checked five or six items, you have a pretty good grounding, and would benefit from refining some of your weak points. If you checked four or fewer items, you likely struggle with finding the balance between Current Performance and Future Potential. This book should help you identify and articulate some clear needs to improve the performance of your organization.

Whatever your score, these statements and questions should help you frame your own needs as you explore the rest of this book for ideas and tips that will help you streamline your own Current Performance while simultaneously building Future Potential.

Chapter 3: Strategy

Chapter 3 describes strategy and the key elements needed to define what makes your organization unique. This chapter poses a fundamental question regarding Current Performance: Given the ways you create value today, what improvements would make it easier for you to create it? These improvements may focus on costs, schedules, quantified tightening of execution, and other fairly well-known success factors. They will tend to be "within the box," operating inside your existing paradigms or approaches.

This chapter also poses a fundamental question regarding Future Potential: Given the ways you hope to create value tomorrow, what new approaches would make it easier for you to create new kinds of value and harder for your competitors to copy? These improvements will be less well-known, and likely won't have clear metrics to evaluate success. They will be risky, experimental, and require investment without easily knowable return, at least for a while. Because of this, they need to be more focused. Start by limiting your list to one or maybe two challenge areas. They will tend to be "out of the box" and will create new paradigms or approaches.

To help you address these questions, read each of the statements below, and check the items that reflect the reality of your organization:

- Our strategy is unique to my organization, and is clearly different from our competitors.
- Our strategy offers clear, actionable plans for improvement and steps for implementation.

- We are aware of environmental and marketplaces changes that will impact the organization.
- We are successfully navigating environmental/marketplace changes.
- My organization or work group generates unique products or services that our customers cannot obtain elsewhere.

Compared to the competition (or our customers' alternatives), we have clear advantages in <u>Current Performance</u>—what it takes to execute—in the following areas:

- Leadership (Leadership is sound, with the right leaders in the right positions to achieve effective execution; it rewards execution of existing plans.)
- Employees (Employees are thriving and highly performing in their respective areas, having the necessary skill sets, training, tools, and environment for performance.)
- Processes (Internal and external procedures are efficient, innovative, high quality, and have effective cost control.)
- Offerings (Offerings to our customers are attractive, with products and services that are currently in demand.)
- Service (Our customer-service orientation and support systems are exceptional; customers feel great when interacting with the organization.)
- Customers (Our customer base is well-defined and loyal, with high levels of cross-selling, up-selling, or repeat business.)

Compared to the competition (or our customers' alternatives), we have clear advantages in <u>Future Potential</u>—what it takes to explore and transform—in the following areas:

- Leadership (Leadership is spending time envisioning, inventing, and communicating the future; it rewards efforts to step back and develop potential.)
- Employees (The organization attracts plenty of highly talented people and can retain the best; it experiments with developing new areas of competence.)
- Processes (Internal and external procedures are agile, allowing for continuous adaptation and improvement.)

- Offerings (We have a healthy "pipeline" of new offerings the market-place will find attractive in the future.)
- Service (We are building our brand with effective marketing, sales, and brand management; service approaches are agile in adapting to new offerings or new customer needs.)
- Customers (Our customers are brand advocates to others and are excited about any new products and services we roll out; we explore new marketplace segments.)

Vital organizations would clearly endorse all of the first five items, at least four of the Current Performance items, and have an undeniable clarity on one or two of the Future Potential items. If all of the Future Potential items were checked, it may reflect too diffuse a strategy: A clear competitive edge across all six aspects of the Vitality Model is unusual and may be unsustainable.

Chapter 4: Leadership

Chapter 4 covers leadership, including how the top team aligns around Vitality and relentlessly embodies and communicates the organization's balance regarding Current Performance and Future Potential.

The first critical question highlighted by this chapter is: How well is the top leadership team aligned around both short-term and long-term needs? This would include general agreement, but also the ability to debate disagreements on specific points constructively. It includes sharing resources and working "across the aisle" between Current Performance and Future Potential. The second question is: How well do the top leaders relentlessly communicate this shared short-term and long-term vision to the entire organization, empowering clear prioritization and investment? To better answer these questions, complete the assessment below by checking the items that reflect the reality of your organization:

- There is a relentless commitment across the leadership team to a vision of Vitality—a balance of streamlining Current Performance and investing in Future Potential.
- There is a clear understanding of which leaders and groups are focused on Current Performance and which ones are focused on Future Potential.
- There is a widely-held confidence in the future of the group and its ability to achieve its vision.

- Leadership-team members are willing to consider, discuss, and implement opposing views; they have general respect for other's opinions.
- Rewards and reinforcements encourage team members to look beyond their unit and work toward both the short- and long-term good of the entire organization. (This can reduce interpersonal competition and facilitate negotiations of budgets and other precious resources.)
- All top leaders speak with "one voice" about the balance of short-term and long-term needs.
- Communications about strategy and overall directions enable those several layers down from the top to set priorities, investing time and resources in efforts aligned with both success today and a thriving tomorrow.

All seven of these items would be present within a vital organization. If you can only check five or six items, then your priorities for improvement are clear. If you checked fewer than five items, your leadership team needs meaningful calibration as your first step in developing Vitality.

Chapter 5: Developing Vital Individuals

Chapter 5 addresses the characteristics of individuals that make them more adapted to executing Current Performance, developing Future Potential, or the boundary-spanning that helps translate potential into performance. The pivotal question suggested by this chapter is: While you may have people focused on delivering on Current Performance, and you might have a few dreamers who think about and conceptualize Future Potential, do you have those critical people who can span the boundary between them? These are the people who understand the dynamics of Current Performance and daily operations, envision viable and relevant ways to invest in Future Potential, and help convert those Future Potential ideas into Current Performance routines. The assessment questions below will help you identify these people and whether your group has the right mix.

First, consider the characteristics of those who operate in a Vitality fashion, the Boundary Spanners who can maintain a foot in both Current Performance and Future Potential. For each of the statements below, begin by evaluating yourself. Check the items that accurately describe you:

- I am very open to trying new ways of doing things, rather than falling back on the tried and true.

- I tend to be optimistic regarding what my organization can accomplish and what the people within it are capable of.
- If I try something and fail, I tend to rebound quickly.
- I learn from my mistakes, quickly charting an alternative path to accomplish goals.
- I get excited about working on solutions to the toughest problems and biggest challenges my organization faces.
- I get energized by interacting with other people, going out of my way to meet and engage with people I previously did not know.
- I look for the best ideas from people on how to accomplish a challenge, whether they are from within or external to my organization.
- I can sense how others are feeling about a topic and am aware of their needs.
- I am able to persuade people to focus upon and achieve specific goals.
- I set goals for myself, both professional learning goals and career-achievement goals.

How many of these ten statements could you check? You would need a clear majority—six or more—to demonstrate a leaning toward being a Boundary Spanner. While it is important for leaders to have this skill, depending on the work you do, perhaps 5–10% of employees in your organization will need to reflect these characteristics as well. Read through the statements again and try to identify some individuals in your organization who would check even seven or more of the items above. These will be your go-to people to help you balance Current Performance and Future Potential. They will help convert the Future Potential explorations into Current Performance execution.

Based on this new understanding of the Boundary Spanners within your organization (or immediate work group), as a second part of this Chap. 5 assessment, check any of the following items that reflect the reality of your organization or your work group specifically:

- We have in place the dedicated and talented people needed in order to meet the current demands of our customers or others who depend on our work (i.e., excellent at delivering Current Performance).
- We have in place the diversity of talent, the people who can envision and pursue new ideas in order to develop the products and services we will need in the future (i.e., excellent at building Future Potential).

- Across all people with varied responsibilities, we have at least 5–10% who could be considered Boundary Spanners (per the 10-item assessment above).
- Managers consistently understand and monitor the current and the future needs of our customers or those who depend on our work.
- Managers, or others in a position to do so, notice and sponsor the best ideas for improvements or innovations in order to move them forward.

Were there any of the five statements above that you left unchecked? If so, any unchecked areas reflect areas and needs to address in order to become Vital.

Chapter 6: Protecting Innovation

Chapter 6 acknowledges the difficulty of sustained innovation, and presents several angles on how to promote and protect efforts to create breakthroughs in Future Potential. The core question posed by this chapter is: Since time and resources devoted to Future Potential are all too often distracted by day-to-day concerns, what special efforts will you make (whether changes in structures, practices, policies, motivation, etc.) in order to protect innovation? This broad question can be broken down in into more specific ones asking about your own experiences regarding innovation, whether "Little i" or "Big I". Your "Big I" innovations to build Future Potential will typically have a shorter, more focused, and maybe more daunting list than your "Little i" innovations to streamline Current Performance. With the statements below, check off all items that apply to your organization:

- We successfully live up to our own innovation aspirations regarding how we streamline Current Performance ("Little i" innovation).
- We successfully live up to our own innovation aspirations regarding how we build Future Potential ("Big I" innovation).
- We have the capacity (people, time, and resources) to act on promising new or innovative ideas.
- Sufficient attention gets devoted to innovation efforts, and is buffered from the press of day-to-day concerns.
- Our organizational structure (including job assignments and formal accountabilities) helps to "protect" innovation efforts sufficiently, yet keeps them aligned with business realities.

- We effectively buy/acquire and integrate innovation (either to streamline Current Performance or build Future Potential), whether through small-scale or more significant acquisition.
- We have successful programs and explicit efforts to protect and nurture innovation (i.e., formal rhythms to regularly set aside time for employees to be creative, free from operational concerns, as opposed to a less effective "go innovate" directive).

Organizations as a whole, or work groups responsible for breakthrough innovation, need to clearly see all seven of these statements in operation. If you endorsed five or six items, then your priorities for improvement are clear. If you checked fewer than five items, your ability to build Future Potential may be compromised. This can be a temporary situation, but would eventually need to be addressed to avoid stagnation.

Chapter 7: Evaluating Vitality

Chapter 7 describes how to evaluate or measure progress in streamlining Current Performance and, more distinctively, in building Future Potential. The core message of this chapter can be distilled into these overarching questions: How well can you evaluate Current Performance and Future Potential? (These will need to look very different.) How can you evaluate the balance of both? What information do you need to manage the cycling of time, resources, and innovations from exploration to execution? Asking and answering these questions will be an on-going effort. The right balance will change over time, and require on-going adjustment. It will be imperfect. But the goal of increasing the Vitality of your organization, division, or work group is absolutely achievable.

To help you address these questions, evaluate the statements below. These first two are pass/fail prerequisite questions. Vital organizations should be able to clearly check off both of the two statements below before moving on:

- We have Current Performance evaluations that are metrics-oriented and based on factors such as efficiencies, speed, cost, or standardization. (These are not simply based on easily available data, but on carefully considered indicators of success.)
- We use a variety of evidence to determine progress in building Future Potential: We do NOT use efficiency, speed, cost, standardization, or long-term financial metrics to evaluate building Future Potential.

If you can agree with both of those prerequisite statements, then move to the next set. You should evaluate your organization or work group on the next three fundamentals regarding Future Potential:

- How we evaluate our Future Potential is unique to our situation. We do not use industry or other benchmarking to judge our progress.
- We evaluate how well we set the stage for breakthroughs in Future Potential (e.g., investments, agility, resilience, or innovation climate)
- We evaluate speed of learning (failing fast) or other specific learning goals with regard to Future Potential.

Finally, these last "advanced" items address how you manage your evaluations over time. These should be addressed after you have a solid foundation based on the fundamentals covered above:

- We evaluate our performance metrics to understand how they relate to outcomes, and to refine the metrics accordingly.
- We review our metrics and evidence-based accountabilities on a regular basis to ensure they support the original intent (and have not spawned mischief or counterproductive side-effects).
- We evaluate how well we eventually convert Future Potential exploration into Current Performance execution.

If you have the prerequisites covered, as well as the fundamentals, congratulations for being able to work on the advanced items. You are well on your way.

Chapter 8: Navigating Change

Chapter 8 creates the foundation for change as it relates to creating a vital organization, and explores what kinds of change are most beneficial. Overall, the question that echoes through the issues covered in the chapter is this: How well do you set the stage for change, whether incremental or dramatic? Change is clearly instrumental in the pursuit of Vitality. Without it, there could be no Future Potential, and certainly no cycle from Future Potential into Current Performance. As discussed in this chapter, Message, Performance, and Future are the three main components needed to successfully create change, but there remains a lot of nuance as to how companies effectively maintain these transitions once they are implemented, as discussed in the following chapter.. For each of the statements below, check the items that reflect the reality of your organization:

- We have a clear change agenda as it relates to streamlining Current Performance (i.e., improving the ways we execute).
- We have a focused change agenda as it relates to building Future Potential (i.e., the exploration and transformation we will invest in to remain a vital organization).
- The Message of changes we undertake is clear and disseminated; we have a shared vocabulary and frequent dialog across the organization for talking about change, improvements, and innovation. In other words, we know what we mean when we talk about such change.
- The Performance demands based on the changes being implemented are met and provided for, the implications of changes we undertake are clear and addressed; and employees have the tools and resources they need to succeed in the changed environment.
- The Future roles of individuals and of the changes we undertake are clear; there is a confidence in our ability to manage the change, and employees understand what change means for them personally and how they will fit into new environment.

Endorsing all five items would be spectacular. Envisioning and clearly articulating the need to change is very difficult, let alone providing the resources to make it happen. The first two reflect the underlying business need, and the last three reflect your discipline in change management.

Chapter 9: Making Change Stick

While Chap. 8 covers the set-up to change (defining, communicating, etc.), Chap. 9 addresses how to make that change stick. Sometimes articulating the change is the easy part (like making a New Year's Resolution to lose weight), yet there are cases when organizations often lose steam and support for change. How will you continue to support change after it is introduced? Is support provided where you most need to provide support, either personally or through other staff or organizational programs: Motivation, Prioritization, Guidance, or Tracking? What specifically will you do in each of those four areas?

Use the following questions to help you evaluate the answers to these broad questions and gauge your ability not just to live up to your own intentions to change, but to help others to live up to theirs as well.

- The change that needs to happen is well-defined for all involved, including classifying it as Current Performance or Future Potential. (See also Chaps. 3, 4, and 8.)
- The evaluation of the change is well-defined for all involved. (See also Chap. 7.)
- The leaders and individuals most responsible for creating this change have been identified. (Potentially evaluate their strengths according to Chap. 5.)
- Accountabilities or assignments have been defined and clarified for those required to participate in creating and sustaining the change.
- There is collective understanding of where the change is most at risk for failure.

  Fundamentally, those with change assignments are very well supported regarding:

  - Motivation (inspire or drive change, and provide a rationale, for all who need to act differently)
  - Prioritization (align the change to the overall strategy and focus on a short list)
  - Guidance (help people know how to act and what steps to take)
  - Tracking (evaluate change to hold people accountable, as well as to learn)

- Creative Nudges (identified and implemented to help the change process along)

Of the ten items above, the first five cover the set-up, and should be the easiest to endorse. The last five will help the change be sustained over time. Without these last, change will fail. Exactly how you define and provide support (or nudges) will vary dramatically based on what you are trying to accomplish.

Chapter 10: Agility and Resiliency

Chapter 10 emphasizes the need to develop the organization's ability to be agile and resilient in the face of change. The core question addressed deals with whether you have the right kinds of adaptability to adjust to unforeseen changes in the environment, as well as to quickly learn from and adjust as you explore Future Potential. To help you break this down in your evaluation, consider the statements below, five covering agility and five covering resilience, and whether they reflect the reality of your organization (these are adapted from Fig. 7.1 in Chap. 7):

Agility

- We actively and widely scan for new information about what is going on.
- We quickly and clearly make sense of ambiguous or uncertain situations.
- We are open to change.
- We take advantage of opportunities quickly.
- We quickly deploy or re-deploy resources to support execution.

Resiliency

- We have clearly defined and widely held values and beliefs.
- We have a strong sense of identity and purpose that can survive anything.
- We have a strong support network of external alliances or partnerships.
- We are expanding our external alliances and partnerships.
- We have "deep pockets"—access to capital and resources to weather anything.

If you can check four or five within each topic area, you do well with each of these topics. If you only checked three, you may have some sound building blocks, but have some work to do. If you can only check one or two within each area, you will have some serious rigidity to overcome.

Chapter 11: Decision-Making

Chapter 11 acknowledges the limitations of our decision-making skills, and highlights some of the biases and heuristics that are natural and usually very useful, but are sometimes problematic in organizational and business life. The questions this chapter suggests deal with the extent to which you and others in your organization are aware of, discuss, and take steps to minimize decision-making errors that may lead you astray. Certainly mental short-cuts cannot, and should not, be eradicated from how we operate, but the checklist below can help you evaluate the extent to which you might be at risk.

How many of the following reflect the reality within your organization or work group?

- We search relentlessly for potentially relevant or new disconfirming—not simply confirming—evidence that our decisions are on target.
- We accept the role in our team of "Chief Contrarian"—someone who tests arguments for why we might be off target.
- We seek diverse, outside opinions to counter our potential overconfidence (e.g., our news and observations do not come from a short list of regular sources).
- We reframe or flip the problem on its head to see if reframing changes our conclusions.
- We avoid the potential for escalation or further emotional investment in faulty decisions engendered by premature "public" commitment.
- The pressure for closure or for agreement with authority on important issues does not overwhelm sound decision-making.
- We devote sufficient time, research, discussion, and attention to major decisions.
- As a group, we have discussed and acknowledged the decision-making biases that put us most at risk.

Decision-making is a complex and varied exercise with both large and small consequences. If you checked six or seven items, then your risk of bias is perhaps manageable. If you checked four or five items, you should spend some focused time evaluating and improving your decision-making approaches. If you checked fewer than four items, you should go back over recent and still-active decisions and evaluate them against new criteria: You may have significant risk. On the other hand, if you checked all eight items, congratulations are in order, but first step back and think deeply as to whether you are biased in your own evaluations of bias. Organizations very rarely are that perfect.

Chapter 12: Global Vitality Potential Assessment

Chapter 12 describes the broad concept of Vitality within a global context. Of course, not every organization has to deal with the challenges of a global footprint. But for those that do, the overarching questions posed by this chapter deal with how you balance the universal qualities of human organizational life with local nuances that may influence your basic leadership approaches. For each of the statements below, check the items that reflect the reality of your organization:

Enhancers

- My organization is sensitive to local business customs as they concern our customers, employees, business partners, and the local community.
- If I walked into any of my organizational locations around the world, they would be recognizable and would feel like they belong to the same organization.
- Each of our organizational locations could be described as vibrant, taking advantage of and celebrating local culture.
- Employees feel valued, excited about what they are accomplishing, and part of the larger organization.
- The ideas utilized for the building of Future Potential can come from anywhere within my organization.
- If someone has a good idea for maximizing Current Performance, they could get attention paid to it no matter where they are located.
- We find and attract the best local talent in each of our locations.
- We identify and recognize individuals for the unique talents that they can contribute to our organization.
- My organization identifies global top talent and places them into positions critical to the organization, regardless of where they come from.
- In my organization, people get exposure to and are developed for opportunities from a global perspective.
- The building of Future Potential in my organization happens in many locations across our enterprise.

Derailers

- My company operates uniformly across the globe and does not adapt to any local needs.
- There is little that differentiates my organization from other local organizations in the countries in which we are located.
- There is no uniform look, feel, or culture across our global organizational locations.

- We try to find good local talent, but it is just are not available in many of our locations.
- There are stories circulating in my company about the short-comings of locals in the various countries in which we operate.
- Senior management positions in overseas locations of my organization are filled by employees from the home country.
- Expatriate senior managers tend to lead according to the standards and practices of their home countries rather than local standards.

Give yourself a +1 score for each Enhancer you checked, and a −1 for each Derailer, and add them together. If your total score is less than +4, you have some clear work to do in managing the breadth of your enterprise. If you scored +5 or more, you are well on your way to operating in a broad and global fashion.

Chapter 13: Evaluating Vitality Stories

Chapter 13 reviews the power of storytelling, how it is important to organizations, and how you might develop your own storytelling discipline. The overarching questions the chapter asks of you are whether there is a clear storytelling tradition within your organization, how the stories that are told impact your efforts to drive Current Performance or build Future Potential, and what your role is in contributing to the overall organizational narrative. To help you evaluate how to address these questions, your own discipline and climate for storytelling can be evaluated by checking the statements below that reflect the reality of your organization:

- Stories, examples, illustrations or metaphors about how your organization improves itself come easily to mind.
- There are told and re-told stories that are about Current Performance—streamlining, cost control, or other improvements to the ways things are already done.
- There are told and re-told stories that are about Future Potential—exploration, breaking new ground, and developing new capabilities.
- People re-tell the stories they hear from leadership, with similar messages being emphasized.
- Stories told by the leadership of your organization are credible and resonate with the audience.

- You consciously look for and develop stories you can tell that relate to organizational improvement or other aspects of what is important for the future. (Some of these will be your re-telling of stories that other leaders tell).
- You actively cultivate the storytelling discipline within yourself.
- You foster constructive storytelling by improving the discipline in others or creating dramatic symbols or audacious organizational events that spawn stories in others.

If you checked six or more items, then your storytelling discipline is better than most, and this is a tool in your toolbox to help improve Vitality. You will be well-positioned to foster the storytelling discipline in others. If you checked four or five items, you should spend some focused time listening for stories and building your own discipline. If you checked fewer than four items, you may not have considered before the power or storytelling, and should find one or two instances you might match to your strategic agenda.

Whatever your score, as you address these questions, think of a new story about either Current Performance or Future Potential that you can tell. Experiment. Try new approaches. Get started tomorrow.

The Online Vitality Self-Assessment

As mentioned at the start of this Appendix, an interactive version of this Vitality Self-Assessment can be found by visiting OV-CVO.com. Evaluating your efforts this way, along with the worksheets and steps found in Chap. 14, will help you develop and refine your own path to Vitality.

APPENDIX B

Big Five Inventory

The Big Five—Public Domain Mini-Marker Inventory by Gerard Saucier, Ph.D., Professor, Department of Psychology, University of Oregon, Eugene

In several places through this book we have mentioned the Big Five personality factors. Here is a short test you can take to asses where you fall on the Big Five personality inventory.

Please use this list of common human traits to describe yourself as accurately as possible. Describe yourself as you see yourself at the present time, not as you wish to be in the future. Describe yourself as you are generally or typically, as compared with other persons you know of the same sex and of roughly your same age. Before each trait, please write a number indicating how accurately that trait describes you, using the following rating scale:

Scoring

Each scale in the inventory has eight items grouped as below show. For the positively scored items, as indicated below, give a score of 1 to 9. The items that are negatively scores should be reverse-scored: 9=1, 8=2, 7=3, 6=4, 5=5, 4=6, 3=7, 2=8, 1=9. Then total up your score for each scale and divide by 8 to arrive at the mean response for items on the given scale. Higher scores indicate that a greater degree of the trait is present.

1	2	3	4	5	6	7	8	9
Extremely Inaccurate	Very Inaccurate	Moderately Inaccurate	Slightly Inaccurate	Neither Inaccurate nor Accurate	Slightly Accurate	Moderately Accurate	Very Accurate	Extremely Accurate

Trait	Score	Trait	Score	Trait	Score	Trait	Score
Bashful		Energetic		Moody		Systematic	
Bold		Envious		Organized		Talkative	
Careless		Extraverted		Philosophical		Temperamental	
Cold		Fretful		Practical		Touchy	
Complex		Harsh		Quiet		Uncreative	
Cooperative		Imaginative		Relaxed		Unenvious	
Creative		Inefficient		Rude		Unintellectual	
Deep		Intellectual		Shy		Unsympathetic	
Disorganized		Jealous		Sloppy		Warm	
Efficient		Kind		Sympathetic		Withdrawn	

Scoring the Factors

I. Extraversion

   Positively Scored: __Talkative, __ Extraverted, __ Bold, __ Energetic

   Negatively Scored: __Shy, __ Quiet, __ Bashful, __Withdrawn

   TOTAL SCORE___/8=

II. Agreeableness

   Positively Scored: __Sympathetic, __Warm, __Kind, __Cooperative

   Negatively Scored: __Cold, __ Unsympathetic, __ Rude, __Harsh

   TOTAL SCORE___/8=

III. Conscientiousness

   Positively Scored: __Organized, __ Efficient, __Systematic, __Practical

   Negatively Scored: __Disorganized, __Sloppy, __Inefficient, __Careless

   TOTAL SCORE___/8=

IV. Emotional Stability

   Positively Scored: __Unenvious, __Relaxed

   Negatively Scored: __Moody, __Jealous, __Temperamental, __ Envious, __Touchy, __ Fretful

   TOTAL SCORE___/8=

V. Intellect or Openness

   Positively Scored: __Creative, __ Imaginative, __Philosophical, __ Intellectual, __ Complex, __ Deep

   Negatively Scored: __Uncreative, __Unintellectual

   TOTAL SCORE___/8=

To learn more about this instrument, and to compare your results against some norms, see http://pages.uoregon.edu/gsaucier/gsau41. htm. This is the website of Gerard Saucier, Ph.D., who graciously makes his mini-marker Big Five inventory available in the public domain.

Index